P9-CBE-551

PRAISE FOR KARL ZINSMEISTER'S

BOOTS ON THE GROUND

"Karl Zinsmeister's splendid report from within the maelstrom of combat demonstrates how the public can benefit when America's superb military is closely observed by a superb reporter."

—George F. Will, news columnist

"The finest, most objective piece of war journalism I've read since Ernie Pyle in World War II. Tells the story after talking to all grades of soldiers. No one else took the time to tell the full story."

—Lt. Col. Burton Poole, USAF, retired

"The most powerfully real 'war experience' I will probably ever have. I applaud its insight, voluminous factual information, the personal stories collected from many soldiers, and especially the discoveries about the power of love in extreme life-and-death situations. Karl Zinsmeister has done an invaluable service to America in getting to the heart and soul of this war."

—Mary Lavato, a soldier's mother

BOOTS
ON THE
GROUND

A Month with the 82nd Airborne in the Battle for Iraq

KARL ZINSMEISTER

St. Martin's Paperbacks

NOTE: If you purchased this book without a cover you should be aware that this book is stolen property. It was reported as "unsold and destroyed" to the publisher, and neither the author nor the publisher has received any payment for this "stripped book."

For ATZ, a loyal trooper

BOOTS ON THE GROUND

Copyright © 2003 by Karl Zinsmeister.

Cover photo by Karl Zinsmeister.

All rights reserved. No part of this book may be used or reproduced in any manner whatsoever without written permission except in the case of brief quotations embodied in critical articles or reviews. For information address St. Martin's Press, 175 Fifth Avenue, New York, NY 10010.

ISBN: 0-312-99608-X
EAN: 80312-99608-6

Printed in the United States of America

St. Martin's Press hardcover edition / September 2003
St. Martin's Paperbacks edition / October 2004

St. Martin's Paperbacks are published by St. Martin's Press, 175 Fifth Avenue, New York, NY 10010.

10 9 8 7 6 5 4 3 2 1

War is an ugly thing, but not the ugliest of things. The decayed and degraded state of moral and patriotic feeling which thinks that nothing is worth war is much worse. The person who has nothing for which he is willing to fight, nothing which is more important than his own personal safety, is a miserable creature and has no chance of being free unless made and kept so by the exertions of better men than himself.

—JOHN STUART MILL

TABLE OF CONTENTS

Contents

Contents

Note: All the photographs in this book were taken in Iraq and Kuwait by the author.

INTO KUWAIT

1

IS ANYTHING WORTH WAR?

MIRACLES

MADISON COUNTY, NEW YORK, MARCH 1—In four days, I have just confirmed with the Pentagon, I will depart for Kuwait.

Amidst the immaculate winter frost of upstate New York—one day this week our digital thermometer announced that it was 7.2 degrees below zero—my wife and I pluck some tickets off our desk, gather up our children, and begin to drive. As we crunch down snowy streets, the tidy nineteenth-century homes of our village glide quietly by. Rounding Cazenovia Lake—now thickly iced, soon to sprout sails—we traverse rolling hillsides as beautiful as any between Ireland and Argentina. Even at this time of year, the woods and pastures are thick with creatures; yesterday I saw a big tom turkey strutting across a frozen field in his odd birdish rhythm.

In twenty-five minutes we enter a Persian palace— our city's grandest theater of the vaudeville era, now glitteringly restored in gold leaf and crystal. Inside, America's sultans of jazz are holding court—New Orleans pianist Ellis Marsalis joined by his four sons: Branford on sax, Wynton behind a trumpet, Delfeayo playing trombone, and Jason at the drums. Father and sons tear into the set, pouring out an emotionally overwhelming mix of virtuosity, passion, precision, and familial love. Even as we settle into bed that evening, our bones and tendons are still vibrating.

The next night my wife and I journey through the same landscape to a very different destination. Entering a fine concert hall for the latest date in our Syracuse Symphony series, we are swept by a lush romantic wave. United States and European composers Korngold, Barber, and Strauss provide the program. The interpretation is by our orchestra's superb polyglot players—Americans with roots in Romania, Korea, Armenia, and many other lands, tightly joined under the baton of our Japanese conductor emeritus.

At intermission, our delightful new friend the concertmaster comes to the edge of the stage to talk, and introduces the brother of one of his violin students. The thirteen-year-old American marvel immediately engages me in political conversation far beyond his years. He is reading Tocqueville, prodigiously, on his own, and has just quoted one of the sage's many eerily prescient observations—about the "Mohammedan" religion's tendency toward violence. Only the dimming houselights can force an end to our chat. On the way to my seat another patron and I discuss recent late-game heroics by the Syracuse basketball team, our valiant hometown gladiators.

Then Strauss's Alpine Symphony bursts forth so vividly I can see the mountain grasses ripple with wind behind my closed eyes, and feel the spray of the waterfall as the composer chronicles his day on a peak. A joyous Haydn oratorio sung by the local university chorale further punctuates the evening. Our gaze is lifted even higher, beyond the mountaintop, all the way to the mover of mountains Himself.

Just another weekend in the fifty-ninth largest city in the United States of America—a remarkable land where freedom, beauty, and opportunity are available in wondrous abundance to all people, every single day.

In the mad scramble to prepare myself, on just a few days notice, for an indefinite-length assignment in an isolated and unprovisioned combat zone, I throw myself at the mercies of modern capitalism and technology. Internet commerce rapidly brings me two plane tickets, a shortwave radio, powerpacks for my computer, and vital memory cards and lithium batteries for my digital camera. Internet sites provide the precise tunings that will make the radio useful in the Middle East, updates on local communicable diseases, and books and online archives that spell out innumerable essential details. A satellite modem is rented and FedExed to give me a communications link even in the most desolate corner of the forsaken land to which I am headed. A colleague acquires two marvelous "flash drives"—plastic wands the size of my pinkie that can be plugged directly into a computer, loaded with hundreds of fresh photographs and thousands of words, then expressed back to Washington, weighing no more than a pencil.

Not only American capitalism but also American government comes through for me under pressure. The public health nurse for our rural county is a homey marvel of professionalism, surprising me with instant details, hot from the U.S. Centers for Disease Control, on exactly which immunizations and malarial and bacterial therapies I will need to stay healthy in the deserts and mountains of the Middle East.

Four days later I walk into the Walter Reed Army Medical Center in Washington, D.C., to be inoculated against smallpox and anthrax, agents Saddam could employ as battle-zone trumps. The attentive care of the military nurses and technicians, and the openness of the doctors from the Army and the National Institutes of Health about the risks and benefits of vaccination, leave me impressed. As bureaucracies go, America's various governmental arms are more benign than any in history.

Back in middle America, I am able to leave my wife and three children alone for a month or two, confident that they will be protected, and not extorted, by the local police. Unlike in many other parts of the world I needn't worry that some competing tribe or religious sect will rampage through my home community in my absence. I can be comfortable that the town government will pipe my family pure water, and that our utility companies will keep our house warm and electrified in winter. I am certain that local and national businesses will make food, and insurance, and gasoline, and all of life's necessities available to them. I can rely on numerous private companies to send them generally trustworthy newspapers, magazines, and radio and Internet reports on the conflict I'll be in the middle of.

Rather prosaic victories, you're thinking. Except of course they aren't. Literally most of the families on this planet *cannot* go to bed confident that these kinds of services and securities will be there when they awake. America's relative peace and abundance, her deep cultural richness, her competence, her fair play, are very much exceptions in human history.

The pleasures and accomplishments and sureties that fill my final days in the United States are minor miracles. We Americans must never take these things for granted, or falter in our determination to defend the economy and government and traditions of living that make them possible. As I think and then type this I am somewhere over the Black Sea, just hours shy of entering a land where none of this—not one single piece—can be counted on.

COSTS

When navigating any airport today, one is sickened by the thought of how much time, motion, and energy must now be wasted simply to fend off the depradations of a tiny band of cruel maniacs: the hordes of new federal employees hired to x-ray, question, rummage, wand, and frisk; the enormous expenditures on explosive-sniffing machines and giant cargo scanners; the squandered time and opportunities represented by millions of travelers shuffling about in boredom, all across the country, when they would rather be doing something productive.

What mighty deeds could this army of workers and mountain of resources have accomplished if applied to some more fruitful task? It's a Kafkaesque waste.

I'm likewise struck by the high price we pay for political terror when I stare at the thick pile of papers that accompanied my biowarfare inoculations—adverse reaction warnings, indemnity forms, wound treatment instructions, on and on, all methodically researched and drawn up, then explained to me by six or seven different individuals. An Army doctor—a highly qualified colonel—spent about forty minutes giving me the briefing that precedes emergency smallpox immunization. I kept thinking guiltily that he should really be doing something more important than clicking through a PowerPoint presentation for an audience of one.

Bright medical professionals in a great many places have recently invested vast amounts of time and money brushing up on prevention, discovery, and treatment of diseases that by rights should be obscure or erased entirely as human dangers. Had these needless threats not been synthesized by vicious terrorists, those men and women could have been solving other knotty problems instead.

For that matter, what would I be doing this spring if the readers of my magazine, and the rest of the world, were focused on something more constructive than war? Certainly not buying airplane tickets to Kuwait for the privilege of sleeping in the dust and eating MREs (military "meals ready to eat" that one friend insists should really stand for "meals refused by Ethiopians").

What would President Bush and the U.S. Congress be taking up this spring absent the mad intemperance of men like Khalid Shaikh Mohammed and Saddam Hussein? I expect we'd be making breakthroughs right now on an historic reform of Social Security, and hammering out new ways to stanch the bleeding at the Medicare program. We'd be further along in figuring out how to help poor people through religious charities rather than just government agencies. And our defense costs would be a lot slimmer, while the Pentagon would be more fully reshaped into nimbleness. (French cheese sales in the United States would also be much stronger.)

But instead of pursuing progress on new frontiers, much of our national attention is now directed, quite literally, to damage control.

Perhaps most significant, our national economy would not now be entering its third year of funk had Osama bin Laden spent more time taking care of his wives and less time destroying other people's families. September 11, and the fear, uncertainty, and distraction that followed, have taken a mighty whack out of U.S. financial vigor. Our powerful economic engine will eventually recover, but today's slumping indicators are much more than just scratches on a stock table; they are symbols of lost opportunities and narrowed horizons for almost every American household.

One personal example of how the black gash on New York City's skyline has fogged landscapes in other parts of America is the school budget in my own hometown. The Twin Towers collapse threw a heavy blanket over New York State's economy, with the result that our upstate school and many others suddenly face large shortfalls in state revenue. This will likely be made up by sharply increasing the property taxes on my house and those of my neighbors. That's terrorism hitting close to home.

Executing war against our assailants is not cheap either. Figures from private and government agencies suggest that the costs of assembling our fighting force in the

Middle East, conducting a month of combat in Iraq, and then bringing the force home again could easily total forty billion dollars or more. Occupying that nation may consume another ten billion dollars through the rest of the year.

Of course the cruelest price of all for Middle Eastern terror is paid in human lives. Saddam is estimated to have killed three million Iraqis since coming to power in 1979, plus hundreds of thousands of Iranians, many Kuwaitis, and some Americans. How many of the soldiers that I befriend on this reporting tour will be injured or killed? How many innocent lives here and around the globe will be ruined or extinguished by future terrorist bombs, plagues, or knives drawn across throats?

There is no painless solution to the devilish costs imposed by the terror masters. But there is a solution: Kill the killers. Quickly. And completely. That's where my campmates, the 82nd Airborne (and company), come in. But first, meet some Kuwaitis.

KUWAIT

KUWAIT CITY, MARCH 6—My first night in Kuwait, the wind began to howl through the downtown hotel towers with such shrieking force that I opened the drapes at about midnight to watch. It was a scirocco, moving with enough force to not only make unearthly noise but also lift tons of fine sand and dust from the vast expanses of desert that surround Kuwait City, and indeed the entire Persian Gulf. Think of a hard blizzard, but of dirt rather than snow. Visibility declined to barely one yard at the storm's peak, forcing drivers to stop dead in the road.

The next morning I got my initial daylight glimpse of the city through a thick brown-gray haze which took nearly a weekend to fully settle. I saw fences and metal roofs on industrial structures that had been ripped away by the winds. And I heard reports from the military public affairs officers that scores of tents had been knocked down at the American Army and Marine camps strung along the Iraq border.

One soldier was stranded, disoriented, in the dust blizzard for three hours while trying to make his way from the mess tent to his sleeping tent. Some carry compasses with them during these short walks to avoid just such a situation. The sand berms that engineers have bulldozed to ring the camps are not just part of the security but also to prevent blinded servicemen from accidentally wandering into the desert during these storms, where they could become lost.

Kuwaitis have opened their doors wide for an American move against Iraq. The antipathy Kuwait feels for its immediate neighbor to the north is such that Iraq is not even listed in Kuwaiti phone books, time-zone guides, or atlases—it has simply been erased as a respectable entity. People bitterly remember the looting and larceny—both petty and grand—committed by the Iraqi occupiers in 1990 and early '91. One businessowner I talked to described how soldiers cleaned out his entire building, stripping not only all of his merchandise but even the furniture and fittings of the office.

Today there is little or no evidence left in Kuwait of this trauma from a decade ago. The country ripples with prosperity and progress, and indeed effects a nearly American standard of living, not only in its central districts but also in outer neighborhoods where I visited supermarkets and teahouses and shopping malls. Many Kuwaitis speak English, and Western products and ideas are ubiquitous. Extensive new buildings glisten in many quarters.

This is not a Western nation, a true democracy (only about one seventh of the population can vote), or a fully capitalist economy (Kuwait's vast oil revenues paper over plenty of economic mistakes). But it is a peaceful and thriving place, where good newspapers are available, where there is no income tax, and where 60 percent of university students and 36 percent of the workforce is made up of women.

Kuwait, like most of the rest of the Persian Gulf states, is now a multicultural nation, where large numbers of imported Filipino, Indian, Sri Lankan, Indonesian, and other workers blend with native Arabs in a tawny skinned, black haired gumbo. Hardly an American-style melting pot (it will be a while before Kuwait has the equivalents of Henry Kissinger, Madeleine Albright, and Colin Powell representing it at international conclaves), but nonetheless a cosmopolitan society where al Qaeda–style intolerance is simply not tenable on a mass basis.

THE BODY ARMOR BAZAAR

With hundreds of thousands of coalition fighting men staging in the country for an invasion of Iraq, Kuwait lies within easy striking range of Saddam's forces. So where do local citizens—and reporters authorized to enter combat with U.S. forces—obtain their protective gear? From a civil defense agency? From the defense ministry?

Try Ahmed al-Saleh and Sons. The thriving family firm, which owns several buildings and a variety of stores, is one of a handful of Kuwaiti businesses that hawks bulletproof helmets, flak jackets, and other military accoutrements. In striving and war-singed Kuwait, the storefronts are much glossier than a typical army surplus store in America, but the contents are much the same.

Want a gas mask? There are eastern European models, and a few made in the West. Don't forget your drinking hose and attachable canteen—vital when you could be spending hours in the desert heat inside the mask and a heavy, impermeable NBC (nuclear/biological/chemical) protective suit. If you wear glasses, I hope you had a prescription insert made. And do buy extra filters. Saddam is not a man given to moderation.

The commonest masks are Korean and Chinese. Do

they work? Probably. Certainly the price is right—perhaps thirty Kuwaiti dinars (around $100), versus two to five times that for competing models. Supplies are a little tight, but not sold out. The Kuwaiti government is suggesting locals place soaked towels around their doors in the event of a gassing, and residents seem remarkably unperturbed. "The U.S. Army will protect us," is the common view.

Battle helmets, on the other hand, are scarce to nonexistent, thanks partly to a run on them by international reporters assigned to "embed" with frontline forces. (Bring your own lifesaving gear.)

One al-Saleh branch, and several other shops as well, tell me they are out of helmets. "Don't worry, we ordered. Soon we have." But "soon" in the Arab souk is five days. Too late. I will be in the desert with the troops by then.

With a little cajoling and pressure, however, the market cracks open a bit. Riyad, the man who insisted no helmets would be available this week, finally pulls a British-made model out of a box. "Just 130 dinar. Usually 165." Only one problem: It already has a bullet hole in it—directly in the forehead, about the size of a round from a 9mm firearm.

I am pleased to note that the shot did not fully penetrate the helmet. But hairline cracks radiate from the hole, and military headgear strikes me as a product category not well-suited to scratch-and-dent sales. I think of a joke a friend told me, just before I left the States, about French tanks: They have six gears in reverse, and one forward (just in case they get attacked from the rear). A helmet with a bullet hole in the forehead but a pristine surface at the back might be best for a soldier or journalist from France, I suggest to Riyad. The comic potential seems to translate surprisingly well.

At another shop, the Kuwait City helmet shortage briefly evaporates. "No problem," says the shopkeeper, who disappears to his storage room, returning with a well-made piece of shiny blue headgear bearing a gummed sticker that reads Bulletproof Helmet. I am dubious, and close inspection reveals a manufacturer's label inside, blacked out with magic marker but still legible, where I can make out Fireman's Helmet. Hmmm. I'd love to follow a firefighter around for a story some day, but I tell my new friend Sharif that this won't do for where I'm going.

Like any good salesman, Sharif shifts gears once he realizes he has a discerning customer. "Come back tomorrow, and I give you choices."

Meanwhile, I try on flak jackets. A model made in Northern Ireland has nice Velcro fittings. But it seems to have been tailored with a bantam border guard named Finbar in mind, not a 6'5" American. Call me sentimental, I mime to my attendant, but I cherish not only my chest but also my abdomen.

I also tell him this feels like police-level Kevlar, not full military gear. At which point he whips out two heavy ceramic plates which he says can be inserted to reinforce the front and rear of the vest. "All special made for you, my friend. Good price."

And Sharif becomes the third shopkeeper to excitedly offer me custom fabric coverings for my gear in "any color camouflage you want." Not seeing any tactical advantage in wearing forest-green camo in a land that makes Arizona look lush, and completely mystified by the distinctive royal-blue wavy pattern printed on lots of Kuwaiti gear, I state my firm though boring preference for straight beige-and-brown desert concealment.

The next day we negotiate the price. I'm offered a free glass of sweet tea, but find that's the only thing I'm going to get at a bargain price, despite some earnest negotiating. If the Kuwaitis are grateful to Americans for saving their bacon back in 1991 it sure doesn't show up in the prices on lifesaving gear offered to this reporter. I'm sorely tempted to walk away. But, hey, I'll never get this story done if I get a hole opened up in my body.

THINKING OF BERLIN

The new and the old, the religious and the secular, the traditional and the modern blend rather seamlessly in Kuwait. Yacob al-Qalaf, whom I met in a teahouse where he sat smoking the age-old hookah pipe in the company of some other men in customary headdress, turned out to be a well-educated professional and speaker of polished English. Kuwait now boasts an excellent system of superhighways. And beside them one still sees goat and camel herds tended by berobed Bedouins who live in desert tents.

Yacoub al-Saleh, who sold me my body armor and then took some interview questions, is the second son in a wealthy trading family, a speaker of exemplary English whose business often takes him to America and other parts of the West. Just the same, he wore the traditional Kuwaiti headdress, and excused himself at one point for forty-five minutes to go pray at a nearby mosque. For more than an hour while I was in his office, his son, perhaps ten years old, chanted his Koran lessons in a loud singsong over in an adjoining room.

Similar meldings of modernity and tradition are successfully underway in Qatar (which has a relatively progressive government that is enterprising, fair to women, tolerant of a mostly free press, and quite friendly to America), Dubai (which has made itself an economic success despite meager oil resources by opening itself to tourism and trade), and other Persian Gulf states. These provide encouragement that the Arab Middle East needn't be an economic desert and human rights swamp for the future.

Could Iraq, under American tutelage, and with renewed links to its gradually modernizing neighbors, follow a similar course? There is good reason to hope. First of all, it is not an ignorant culture. Iraq was traditionally the intellectual center of the Arab world. This is the land of Hammurabi, the society that introduced the concept of zero into mathematics, the home of the singer of the *Gilgamesh Epic*.

Iraqis are described by experts as having an "unquenchable thirst for knowledge," and at one point boasted the highest rate of Ph.D. holders in the world. In the later 1970s, before Saddam Hussein seized power, the number of students in technical fields soared; great progress was made against disease; and the rights of women were established as nowhere else in the Arab world. Among the estimated five million Iraqis who are now political refugees and economic expatriates living abroad, there is a great store of knowledge and experience. If they were to return, this could help jump-start their land into the club of successful nations.

Iraq certainly has a fighting chance. It retains much less of the medieval baggage that weighs down people like the Saudis and the Afghans. Still, making Iraq over will not be simple, for this is a portion of the world without humane political traditions. It is sobering to note that the Iraqi government has been overthrown twenty-three times since 1920.

After making that an even two dozen, America will try to help the Iraqis put an end to their ugly political history. The United States has done it before—directly in places like Japan and Germany, and indirectly in places like eastern Europe and Latin America, where decades of dogged effort finally shoved those societies away from dictatorship and toward representative free enterprise.

The fond vision of any sensible American is that the

remaking of Iraq will launch a kind of Berlin Wall syndrome in the long-accursed Middle East. A decade and a half ago, who could have guessed how rapidly other Iron Curtain nations would embrace freedom once it started to flicker in the heart of the Soviet bloc? Could a free and prosperous Iraq have an equally revolutionary effect on its neighbors?

Tyrants like Yasser Arafat and Syrian president Bashar Assad have already felt the winds blowing and made efforts to dodge and preempt the freedom spirit with cosmetic softenings. Iran is actively bubbling with liberation sentiments, and could well throw off its mullahs within a blink if an attractive model of modernity can be launched in Iraq. This is a grand and uncertain vision, but worth all effort. Redirecting the Middle East away from its self-immolating narrowness would be the accomplishment of a lifetime—and very possibly the difference between America's safety over the next two decades and a terrorist holocaust of truly historic dimensions.

SADDAM'S GANG

Many of the cruelest dictators across the ages were fatherless offspring of disordered families. That was Adolf Hitler's background, and it is also Saddam Hussein's. Saddam's father abandoned him before he was born. His penniless mother went to her brother's house near the city of Tikrit to give birth, and then in turn abandoned the baby, leaving him to be raised by his uncle's family. They gave him a name which means "clasher" or "one who confronts."

Iraq is a tribal society. There are 150 different alliances of family clans. Most are highly interbred and insular. Fitting this pattern, Saddam married his cousin Sajida Talfah in 1963, and sired sons Uday and then Qusay.

The more one studies Saddam Hussein's ruling circle, the more it looks like a gang rather than a government. He stuffed the ruling ranks with his relatives and fellow members of the Tikrit-based tribe to which he belongs. When Saddam took over the country in the late 1970s, all of the most powerful men in his ruling Baath party were members of the Talfah family of Tikrit. To disguise the extent to which one small clan dominated affairs of state the party actually abolished surnames, requiring that ID cards record only a child's first name and the name of his father. Even today, half or more of the top Iraqi leaders are cousins or other relatives of Saddam.

Saddam originally groomed his eldest son Uday as his successor, but the boy's psychopathic violence eventually proved him unfit even by current Iraqi standards. One of Uday's "hobbies" is selecting women on the street to rape and kill. He circulates sadistic videotapes to friends and associates showing him torturing enemies to death. His drunken orgies and violence are legendary.

The son reflects what his father taught him. Saddam started taking Uday to executions of dissidents when he was five. As a ten-year-old the youngster began watching torture sessions. After Uday murdered a member of Saddam's entourage in one of his fits of drunkenness and mental instability, though, he lost the mantle of presidential successor to his brother.

Number two son Qusay, a couple of years junior at age 36, is now Saddam's heir apparent. Qusay is in charge of intelligence and security in Iraq (the only growth industry in this police state), and also head of the Republican Guard. He and his brother sit at the top of a list of Saddam's most abusive lackeys slated for capture and trial, or elimination, if American or British forces can locate them.

Currently, Uday runs much of Iraq's media. He is also head of the national press union, which—what a coincidence!—named him "journalist of the century" for his "innovative role, his efficient contribution in the service of Iraq's media family . . . and his defense of honest and committed speech." Recently, *Babel*, one of the newspapers Uday uses to toady for his father, has spent much of its time praising "peace" demonstrators in the West for inflicting "humiliating international isolation" on the United States and Britain. Leafing through issues of this and other Iraqi newspapers published just before the war I see numerous photos of the "No War on Iraq" rallies being staged in places like San Francisco and Berlin.

Recognizing that Saddam's best chance—really, only chance—for surviving America's military wrath is to stall for time (for which the U.N. inspection process proved perfectly suited), and then hope that peaceniks in the West will eventually sap U.S. determination to remove his father, the younger Hussein's *Babel* praised the protestors of Europe and America for opening "a new chapter in the global balance of power." Hardly a pacifist himself, however, Uday is personally in control of several Iraqi militias.

Bellicosity has been Saddam Hussein's trademark right from the start. His first prominent public act was to plot to kill his nation's leader at the time, Abdul Karim Qasim. Within a year of becoming president himself in 1979, Saddam had dragged his country into a war with Iran that lasted eight years and killed 435,000 people. During that period, the Iraqi used chemical weapons against soldiers and civilians on at least forty different occasions. Two years after that disastrous adventure came to a close, he invaded Kuwait, bringing more destruction, defeat, and death to his people.

Saddam's willingness to inflict suffering on his own nation apparently knows no bounds. While only around three thousand Iraqi civilians were killed in Desert Storm (thanks to the care of American and allied military leaders), Saddam's brutality in quelling the internal uprisings that followed in fourteen out of the country's eighteen governates (plus his neglect of basic health services) took fully 105,000 lives in the war's aftermath. When the U.S. and Britain proposed in 2001 to ease the life of everyday Iraqis by loosening sanctions on civilian goods in return for tighter controls on arms, Saddam dismissed the offer, further pauperizing his people to keep his grip on power.

Today, incomes in Iraq have tumbled to a tenth or less of their levels two decades ago. A quarter of all school children no longer attend elementary school. Basic commodities like water have become so scarce that building lobbies are now sometimes mopped with fuel oil instead. (That is something Iraq will never run short of.)

In addition to the estimated three million Iraqi citizens he has killed, Saddam has driven four to five million people (15 percent of the population) into exile abroad. There are now about eighty different anti-Saddam parties operating throughout the Middle East, in London and other European capitals, and in the United States. This man is an expert at making enemies.

The misery Saddam has been so willing to make his countrymen bear ends at his palace door. Saddam's personal wealth, all accumulated through state graft, is now reliably believed to total around thirty-two billion dollars. On the day I write this, there are reports in the Kuwaiti papers that Saddam has just dispatched his personal jeweler to Thailand to buy him millions of dollars worth of diamonds, presumably for him to live off of should U.S. forces put him on the run.

———

Quite literally nothing is sacred to Iraq's tyrant. A Defense Department briefing just before I left Washington presented photographs of ammunition dumps, anti-aircraft guns, and other military equipment recently relocated next to schools, hospitals, mosques, shopping centers, and other sensitive positions in an attempt to either play on American sympathy to prevent the war material from being destroyed, or else foment an international uproar if inadvertent damage is done in the course of bombing it.

Saddam is determined to repeat his successes of the first Gulf War, when he did this notoriously. In one incident, he had his forces shear the dome off the Basra mosque and claim it was done by an allied bomber, when in fact the nearest bomb craters were hundreds of yards away. A famous 1991 aerial photograph of the Ziggurat of Ur (a four thousand-year-old religious pyramid located in the ancient city which produced the biblical patriarch Abraham) shows two MiG-21 jets parked almost touching its stonework. They were trucked there to be sheltered by U.S. unwillingness to desecrate the site, and indeed they were spared during the bombing.

Even more heinous is Saddam's predilection for using innocent humans to shield his forces. The most remembered example of this in the last Iraq war was the al-Amiriya incident, where civilians were invited by the Iraqis to use the first floor of a bunker—whose lower levels sheltered a command-and-control center—as housing. Unaware of the civilian presence, U.S. warplanes destroyed the bunker, resulting in more than one hundred deaths, an uproar in Europe, and a pullback in American attacks.

Encouraged by the mobilizations of the Western peace movement, Saddam and his henchmen hope to create more such "strategic incidents" this time around. The idea remains that media-viewer outrage might cause military planners to get cold feet and put an end to their raids. As part of this, the Iraqis welcomed some two hundred antiwar activists from foreign countries into Iraq to serve as "human shields."

As hostilities approached, some of these shielders realized that their Iraqi sponsors were placing them around military and industrial facilities rather than the hospitals, schools, and other such locales they imagined they would occupy, and some hesitantly complained. Meanwhile, the U.S. Department of Defense warned that by volunteering to serve Saddam Hussein, the shielders may have crossed the line between "noncombatant" and "combatant." Could this be a case of "Live by TV imagery, die by TV imagery"?

2

BATTLE STATIONS

OUR NATIONAL SWAT TEAM

CAMP CHAMPION, KUWAIT, MARCH 12—Two or three hours after the Twin Towers collapsed, the 82nd Airborne Division rolled their equipment out onto the pavement down in Fort Bragg, North Carolina. "We thought we might be going somewhere. We were ready to move that day," says Captain Jose Reyes, a 30-year-old Tex-Mex product of the ROTC program at UT Austin, and a proud partisan of his Lone Star State.

The 82nd is the only major military force in the country in a position to do that. Instant response to crimes against the nation is their bread and butter. There are Marine expeditionary forces trained and equipped to move rapidly, but not as fast as the 82nd can get infantry, artillery, vehicles, and armed helicopters into an airplane with its wheels up, headed anywhere on the globe.

Only about a third of the 82nd Airborne has come to the Persian Gulf. Another third is in Afghanistan right now, pursuing an expanded campaign against Taliban and al Qaeda remnants along the Pakistani border. The final third of the division has just rotated back home to Fort Bragg after an earlier tour among the Afghans.

The Army's other airborne division, the 101st, is also a light, transportable fighting force, but very different. They ride helicopters into battle—squadrons of Black Hawks, among others. That's fine if the division is already sitting within a few hundred miles of the hot zone. But flying wedges of helicopters can generally leap only one hundred to two hundred miles at a bound. Then they must land to refuel, let their security perimeter catch up, and regroup. So if you need to get thousands of infantrymen plus their associated artillery, helicopters, and fighting and engineering vehicles any significant distance from a base, and you don't have time to wait for snail-paced transport ships, or tortoise-paced convoys or airlift, there is only one alternative: the 82nd.

Here's how they do it: For every two or three thousand fighting men you need on the ground, take sixty to seventy communications trucks, gun jeeps, ammunition trailers, and construction vehicles (including a dump truck and a bulldozer for rebuilding a blasted airfield on the fly), and pack them on large pallets with stacks of shock-absorbing cardboard inserted under key pressure points. Then, within hours of any call from the president, these soldiers and this gear will pile into C-130 or C-17 transports, and fly to wherever the bad guys live.

When the site to be seized comes into range, the backs of the planes will be opened and small pilot chutes will be thrown out. The tie-downs on the pallet-packed jeeps and bulldozers will be removed. Then the mini-chutes will be allowed to pull out large main parachutes. When these fill with air, it's good night Irene: The trucks are whipped out of the gaping transport with a teeth-rattling roar.

Within minutes, paratroopers follow the vehicles out the rear doors and into the darkness (troopers almost always jump and fight in pitch black now, where U.S. night-vision technology gives them powerful advantages over adversaries). The soldiers come in carefully chore-ographed order—artillery teams placed near their how-itzers, the engineers by their trucks, riflemen around the perimeter.

Each trooper will be strapped to a twenty-five-pound parachute. He'll wear body armor and a ballistic helmet weighing perhaps twenty pounds. His weapon (rifle, machine gun, grenade launcher) will add another twenty pounds, and he'll have forty-five pounds of ammo, food, water, night-vision gear, and other equipment in his rucksack. As soon as they've landed and stowed their chutes, task one for these men is to zap any bad guys and secure the drop zone—because wave two is already on the way.

Within a blink, more C-130s and C-17s begin to land within the perimeter protected by the first jumpers. All it takes, in a pinch, is two to three thousand feet of firm dirt, grass, or hard sand, and the dance is on. The very first few birds disengorge an especially exotic cargo: armed Kiowa helicopters (two, wedged head to tail, per school-bus-sized C-130 bay, or seven inside each C-17). If the landing zone is hot, each Kiowa's seven-man crew can have its fins reattached, its rotor blades locked, and the turbine winding with both pilots strapped into their seats within a half hour.

"Infantry guys feel much better as soon as we see them go up," one soldier told me. For the Kiowas serve as modern-day equivalents of horse cavalry: eyes up in the air to scout out threats (and send back voice and picture images of what lies over the horizon), plus a light-weapons package sufficient to stop anything from two tanks (two Hellfire laser-guided missiles), to a mass of charging soldiers (seven 2.75-inch rockets and a .50 caliber machine gun).

The helicopters work closely in pairs or groups of four. I'm bunking with the First Battalion Kiowa pilots and crews. It's a smart, sharp, and close-knit group. They're known as the Wolfpack.

CAMP CHAMPION

Five weeks ago, what is now called Camp Champion was a sandy plot on the fringe of Kuwait International Airport. Today it's a tight little city of maybe eighty very large rented Bedouin tents connected by gravel paths, each capable of holding about fifty men or women (there are perhaps one hundred women among the 3,320 soldiers now calling the camp home). Outside each tent is a Scud bunker—a long precast concrete arch layered with sandbags laboriously filled by soldiers under a midday sun. In the event the camp comes under attack, we'll all don our gas masks and dive under the four-foot tall shelters.

Security is tight. Stern MPs check IDs three times before allowing entry. Concrete barriers and concertina wire ring the acreage, and there are pillboxes at the corners and gates. Military secrecy forbids me or the other six reporters embedded with the 82nd from mentioning, or photographing, our Kuwait Airport location in stories we file during the lead-up to battle.

The territory occupied by the Signal Corps prickles with a forest of antennas. There is also a rudimentary sick tent, and a Morale, Welfare, and Recreation tent equipped with Ping-Pong, weight sets, and other distractions. There is a massive soft-walled mess hall where chow is served eight hours per day.

A canvas chapel is kept busy with services and Bible studies throughout each evening. When the troops first arrived there was a surge of demand for baptisms. Chaplains built a hot-tub–sized font out of sandbags, put in a plastic liner, and filled it with water for a goodly number of immersions. Some were first-timers, a chaplain told me; others were renewing their commitments.

The place is a beehive of activity. Day and night, soldiers, pilots, and maintenance workers come and go through the tents as they rotate shifts. There is a constant rumble of trucks, forklifts, and six-wheeled gators. From very low overhead comes a continuous roar of airplanes and helicopters—mostly large military cargo planes ferrying in the mountain of supplies required to provision an army of a quarter-million souls.

There is the lawn-mowing buzz of the C-130's four giant propellers, the hushed jet swish of the intermediate-sized and very high-tech C-17, and the unearthly buzzing whistle that distinguishes the gigantic C-5 as it lumbers up into the heavens, a veritable giraffe-dodo-hippo of floating improbability. Layered on top of this are periodic *thwack-thwack-thwacks* from Chinook and Black Hawk helicopters, and the high streaking roars of supersonic fighters. Nonstop. I've always smilingly told my children to think of military jet noise as "the sound of freedom." Here it is that, and also the sound of insomnia.

I have the run of the camp, and further tours reveal a polebarn popped up by the engineers (where vehicles get packed on pallets for airdrops), a good-sized lumberyard, and rows and rows of steel shipping containers filled with almost every supply imaginable, all of this ferried about by a green herd of forklifts. Around the camp's perimeter, hundreds of vehicles are carefully staged in the order in which they'll roll into transport planes or convoys. Phalanxes of chemical porta-johns ring the fringes of the camp, along with dispensers of liquid hand sanitizer to keep dysentery down. A few modular buildings contain the post's only running water—a limited number of shaving sinks and some welcome warm showers.

Even in early spring the desert gets quite warm during the day, yet remains cold at night. The dust storms hit about once a week, filling every cranny of each tent, pack, sleeping bag, camera, computer, and body with a fine, lightly brown, distinctively dirt-scented grit. Lungs and nasal passages sting, wheeze, and swell. It's impossible to keep clean, but most of the soldiers bear up like, well, troopers.

The old-timers know it could be a lot worse. Back in 1991, when the 82nd Airborne rushed into the sands of Arabia to discourage Saddam Hussein from rolling his army beyond Kuwait and into the Saudi kingdom, the desert living conditions were miserable. There was no running water for months, no cooked food, poor shelter, and no relief from brutal summer heat. I've overheard veterans of that deployment talk about going two or three months without a proper wash or hot meal.

This camp is vastly more humane than its predecessor

of twelve years earlier. And one of the major reasons is the Army's new preference for private civilian contractors. Most of the nonmilitary operations here in Camp Champion—rental and erection of the tents, operation of the mess facility, foodstuff purchases, maintenance of the showers and porta-johns, laundry, the PX shop, garbage pickup—are run by private companies organized by lead contractor Kellogg, Brown & Root, a division of the Halliburton company.

Brookings Institution scholar Peter Singer now counts hundreds of firms that specialize in military contracting, which has become a global two hundred billion dollar annual business. At some point the Pentagon discovered that letting the private sector handle these tasks instead of doing them with military manpower would not only save money but also result in a higher quality service.

It isn't just construction and domestic services that are being contracted out, but also complex computer assistance, water and sewage management, even weapons training and personal security. The bodyguards the Defense Department hired to take over protection of Afghan president Hamid Karzai are civilian contractors (DynCorp), as are the specialists selected to train and equip the new Bosnian Army (MPRI), and the people de-mining the Bagram air base in Afghanistan (RONCO).

LEG LAND

"I'd get my eardrums ripped if I walked around like these guys," observes one airborne soldier, a personable Hispanic from California, as we stroll, on a postal errand, through an adjoining camp that houses regular Army and National Guard troops. Such camps are referred to (somewhat derisively) as "Leg Land," and such soldiers as "Legs," by the elite Airborne soldiers used to winging rather than walking their way into conflicts. (Of course, intra-Army rivalries are nothing compared to the competition with other service branches. One choice bit of latrine grafitti I notice on the wall above a pit toilet reads: Shhh! Baby Marines hatching—with an arrow pointing directly into the nearly full pit.)

At Arifjan, another post I visited which is one of the Army's major logistical centers in Kuwait, the personnel are almost all supply-chain staffers and other nonfighters, part of the massive "tail" that follows the "tooth" portion of our military beast. The atmosphere here is comparatively lax. Soldiers wander about without their gas masks, in motley clothing, shirttails hanging. The word in the tents of Camp Champion is that seventy-five pregnant female soldiers have recently been pulled out of Arifjan. I don't try to confirm this, but it doesn't seem implausible. Pregnancy epidemics have indeed swept other corners of the American military where loose discipline and easy fraternization of the sexes have been allowed to root. The naval repair ship USS *Acadia* had a scandalous thirty-six female sailors return home pregnant during its seven-month sea tour amidst the first Gulf War.

Among the airborne of Camp Champion, however, the uniforms are sharp, the bodies are hard, and the discipline is tight. "You have to volunteer twice to get here," they tell me, "once to join the Army and once to become a paratrooper." Here, officers are saluted on the street. A soldier doesn't step foot outside his tent without his rifle or machine gun slung over a shoulder, or without a complete uniform of battle fatigues. If he wanders any distance he'll definitely be wearing his body armor and ballistic helmet (the "Dome of Discipline," as it is known). No one goes anyplace without his gas mask. And leaving the area requires strapping a rucksack on your back holding a full NBC suit (fifteen pounds of protection from nuclear/biological/chemical attack).

I get extensive training, like everyone else in camp, in techniques for surviving NBC warfare. It takes a few hours to learn how to don, clear, and seal a gas mask in eight seconds, and quickly self-inject the three doses of atropine antidote that each of us carry at all times in case of a nerve agent gassing. We also carry a strong anticonvulsant to administer to buddies already on the ground. We've been trained how to decontaminate our exposed skin with charcoal powder, how to drink from a canteen while wearing a gas mask with the special built-in hose, and how to carefully change out of one contaminated suit and slip on a new one.

As the risk of chemical or biological attack increases, due to physical proximity or battle escalation, more and more gear must be piled on. First the coat and pants. Then the rubber boots and rubber gloves. Finally the gas mask and hood. It's definitely possible to fight in all this gear, but you'd better not be claustrophobic, and exposure to the hot sun is a brutal experience.

PRACTICE MAKES PERFECT

MARCH 17—Today is the "expiration date" of President Bush's original warning to Saddam Hussein, and it's safe to say that the rank and file in Camp Champion are chomping at the bit to get the Iraqi strongman into either a new career or a fresh grave. "Soldiers, who do the fighting, are generally not enthusiasts for war. But our people are convinced they have an important job to do here, and they want at it," says strapping 6'6" Colonel Arnold Bray, who as commander of the 325th Regiment is "boss" to about 80 percent of the men and women here. When Colin Powell announced to the world this evening that the United States and its allies were withdrawing their resolution before the obstreperous U.N. Security Council, and that "the time for diplomacy has come to an end," riotous cheers rippled through the vast mess hall where soldiers of the 82nd packed in to watch the news on a big-screen TV.

Of course it takes more than discipline, more than

enthusiasm, more than ferocity to make an effective fighting force. There are countless technical and physical skills to be mastered, long mental checklists to run through, and the students are mostly young males with short attention spans. All day and night, throughout the camp and on firing ranges and airstrips way beyond its borders, there is teaching, practice, mentoring, and fanny whacking going on.

Infantry cross training on different weapons. A slideshow on identifying mines and booby traps. Lots of brushing up on mortar fire. Endless repetition of jumping out of trucks and helicopters to set up security perimeters. Tutorials on how to shout "Halt!" "Drop your weapons!" and "Who is in charge?" in reasonably accented Arabic.

Plus dogged physical training of all sorts: Improvised weightlifting, running, calisthenics, chin-ups, teams of six pushing out-of-gear trucks up and down dirt paths. As Colonel Bray put it in one conversation, "Infantrymen are pack mules, not race horses. We spend a lot of time building body strength to make sure they can carry whatever needs to be brought to the battlefield."

Meanwhile, supply masters carefully calculate plane loads and queue up vehicles. Helo pilots practice flying in dust and at night. And everybody undergoes regular review of the procedures necessary to avoid injury when jumping out of a perfectly good airplane with a heavy load on one's back.

There are many reminders that today's high-tech warfare is not easy, not automatic, not something that just happens on a pushbutton basis (as the public occasionally seems to imagine). The process of speed-loading helicopters onto transport planes turns out to be not so speedy on the day I observe it being practiced. Another day, infantrymen arrayed across a parking lot in the prone rifle position are stacked up in a fashion that could lead to one soldier popping another in the back. When I visit an anti-aircraft battery responsible for keeping hostile planes and missiles away from the 82nd, they're having trouble reading the squawk boxes that are mounted on each friendly helicopter. Make a misidentification in battle and you could either launch a Stinger missile at a U.S. pilot or let a bad guy fly right into your lap.

I get up at 0300 to accompany a howitzer team to the artillery range, where they test their ranging procedures and then lob some heavy 105mm punches over the horizon in a series of gut-sucking thuds. The "six minute drill" intended to quickly prep the howitzer for firing features a little Keystone-Cop bumping and fumbling, some erase and redraw over at the plotting table, and way too much delay to stop any charging horde. These are all glitches that need to be worked out through concentrated repetition.

But the most serious problem I see is no fault of the young soldiers-in-training: The shells being used by the artillerymen in today's exercise were manufactured in May 1970 (it's stamped right on the containers). And about one shell out of four is defective. Seven bags of explosive propellant come with each shell; the distance the warhead travels is controlled partly by subtracting or adding powder bags. But some of these thirty-three-year-old bags have dry-rotted, and their contents spill onto the sand when they are unpacked, making them useless.

I tell Colonel Bray, who has accompanied us on this training trip, that it seems a shame the firing team has to rely on shells older than anyone on the squad. He replies diplomatically that our Army is expensive, and U.S. taxpayers have been generous; sometimes there are just constraints the troops have to work around. It's decided in the end to use the antique shells only for training. Newer munitions will be rotated forward for use in battle.

TEENAGE BURDENS

MARCH 18—Today some teenage paratroopers from the division's 325th Regiment got a taste of life and death decision making.

Amidst intensified campwide training during the final countdown to action, these soldiers are run through full-dress scenarios, platoon by platoon, very like those they may face in real life within days. In one, a squad simulates a helicopter drop into a hot zone where a friendly

Humvee has just been attacked. Their mission is to secure a perimeter and then evacuate the wounded Americans.

All is proceeding well until a mob of "Iraqis"—actually other soldiers from the same company, wearing desert fatigues but no body armor or helmets—swarm out of an alley between some nearby tents. The role players menace the U.S. soldiers, shouting taunts and throwing a few rocks.

Suddenly one Iraqi in the middle of the pack unslings a rifle that had been hidden behind his shoulder, and attempts to fire. An alert infantryman drops him with a single round (in this case, a shouted "bang"). Unfortunately, the rest of the crowd doesn't flee when the shot rings out, reacting instead with rage. "You killed my brother," shout several of the hostiles, rushing the kneeling perimeter guards.

Chaos breaks out. Additional shots are fired. "You want more? Who wants more?" yells one adrenaline-filled U.S. soldier at his enemies. In the end, four foolish but unarmed civilians lay on the ground, dead.

At the end, all Charlie Company troopers gather around the experienced Rangers and Special Forces officers leading the exercise. "You're freaking going to jail," one interjects, forcefully pointing at the rescue squad. "You have to escalate force gradually. First you shout. Then you show your weapon. Then you shove. Only then do you shoot. You've got dead civilians without any lethal weapons on them. You've got a mess."

"There are going to be tragedies," emphasizes another. "But we've got to avoid atrocities."

The soldiers of the 82nd Airborne are highly disciplined. But there is plenty of room in their ranks for consultation and debate. Immediately after the sergeants speak, a spirited (yet civil) group argument breaks out over whether the squad had any alternative.

"We're in a place where the enemy has just attacked a friendly vehicle and shot two of our guys. Now they're swarming us, and not halting when we tell them to stop, even with us hollering 'kif' [a tidbit of the phonetic Arabic that soldiers in Kuwait are being taught]. I'm sorry, but they're gonna get popped. And we're gonna be able to bring all of our guys home alive," the squad leader says with heat.

"First Sergeant," explains one private who pulled his trigger, "the guy touched my rifle. Which cost $500," he adds with a broad smile, no doubt parroting information loudly driven into his skull by some drill instructor.

"That's different. Under the rules of engagement your rifle is one of your 'sensitive items' and if someone grabs it you're justified in shooting."

The company breaks into smaller groups to further chew over the lessons of the morning's training, and the emphatic debates continue. Most of the infantrymen and squad leaders argue they must err on the side of keeping their men safe. "We're not just waxing people. That's wrong. But listen up: The rules have changed since September 11," a lieutenant suggests. "There are people out there willing to commit suicide. We can't let them near us."

One of the trainers tries to slow the train of sentiment. "Imagine you're at home, and soldiers shoot civilians. What are you gonna think then? Cops have to work through this all the time."

An immediate answer zips back: "Sir, civilians shouldn't be messing around with armed soldiers in an area where we got casualties."

These lightning-fast decisions would be difficult for even Solomon to deliberate all the way through. For teenaged men facing possible death in a hostile country, the choices are hellishly tough. In a scenario run immediately after the one I've just described, four GIs get shot because some nonuniformed Iraqi attackers weren't taken out quickly enough.

Invasion and occupation of Iraq is going to involve lots of raw military/civilian interaction. Defense intelligence shows that Saddam is secreting fighters and dangerous targets thick in the midst of innocent civilians even as I write. Sorting out the two populations is going to be terrifically difficult, and second-guessers in Europe and America will pounce on every mistake and hard case.

The encouraging news is, the men of the 82nd Airborne, and lots of other American fighters, are wrestling energetically with these devilish choices. In sharp specifics, amidst rippling informed argument, they are trying to think their way through the snap decisions that can make the difference between justice and tragedy in wartime. Let's hope that when bullets start to fly the Americans back home appreciate the difficulty of their burden.

THE MILITARY-MEDIA GAP

The embedding effort which has allowed journalists of all stripes to inveigle themselves deep into the bowels of America's military machine in the midst of a major war—including correspondents from al-Jazeera, French TV, and other often anti-American outlets—is like nothing I've ever seen before. No major corporation, no educational institution, no other agency of government has ever invited me and other reporters into their war councils (literally), let me read their secret memos, given me unfettered twenty-four-hour access to their workplaces and employees. It's a tremendously brave gamble on the part of our Defense Department.

The experiment has paid off in many ways. Being shot at together will inevitably give reporters fresh respect for soldiers. And observing the sheer physical and mental stamina required of military men and women during wartime has been an eye-opener for many in the media. Meanwhile, the American public has gotten some reasonably good, very immediate coverage of this war. Indeed, I can tell you that military leaders themselves are reading and watching the reports from embedded reporters, and quite often learning something for the first time in this way. Assuming quality control is reasonable, more information is almost always better than less.

There *have* been a couple of media brain freezes. For example, Fox TV's Geraldo Rivera tried to embed with the other half dozen of us who are reporting with the 82nd Airborne Division. He was turned down. But then the 101st Airborne accepted him. Within a few days he broadcast, live, several of the unit's combat destinations, while the fray was raging, which of course can kill people. He was subsequently thrown out.

Alas, I must state that there are hordes of lightweight reporters here (the highly visible TV correspondents are among the worst). Many came not knowing a howitzer from a ham sandwich, and haven't been asking any of the questions that could lift their veil of ignorance. I'm truly astonished how little homework most reporters did before leaving home—not even learning the very basics like military rank structures so they'll know when they're talking to a mover and when to a shaker. I've observed some laughably wrong and foolish reporting that, had it taken place on a stock trading floor or Senate lobby, would have been instantly spotted in the editorial room as incompetent. But in most editorial rooms these days there's nobody who knows or cares enough about the military to recognize wartime journalistic malpractice.

Some media outlets made wise and careful choices as

to whom they sent to Iraq. Fox, for instance, embedded Greg Kelly, a correspondent who is himself a Marine reservist, with the Army's 3rd Infantry Division. He hit the ground running in terms of shop knowledge, and enjoyed instant credibility with both his military informants and viewers.

But I'm here to tell you that most of the media embeds are just run-of-the-mill reporters. Meaning . . . well . . . that most of them are left-wing, cynical, wiseguy Ivy League types, many with a high prima donna quotient. There are numerous studies showing that members of the major media are now nearly as out of the mainstream politically and culturally as university professors. And that's who I've been seeing in a month in Iraq and Kuwait among the 82nd Airborne.

I have found that a lot of soldiers start out suspicious of reporters. And given the major media's checkered record of interaction with the military, who can blame them? Alas, I'm not seeing enough effort by reporters here to earn their trust.

Many of the journalists observable in this war theater are bursting with knee-jerk suspicions and antagonisms for the warriors all around them. This is aggravated by their tendency to club together, passing far too much of their desert sojourn gossiping with fellow reporters, mocking military mores in snide jokes and wiseguy observations, chafing at the little disciplines required by the military's life-and-death work, banding off as a group to watch DVDs on their computers in the evening, ganging separately in the mess hall during meals, rolling their eyes at each other when ideas like honor, sacrifice, or duty enter the conversation, and otherwise failing to take advantage of this unparalleled opportunity to enter deeply and perhaps sympathetically into the lives and minds of superlative fighting men.

I know there are a few journalists present here, like Michael Kelly of *The Atlantic*, who support this intervention by our commander in chief, and the troops carrying it out. And some of those I've met could not be clearly categorized on the basis of gentle questioning of their views. But I can inform you that the vast number of the reporters I've spoken to are scornful of this war's aims and execution.

In the first days of battle, the only thing that got the sustained respect and attention of the fellow scribes I'm bumping into each day was the apparent death of three TV journalists on March 22. At a lower level, there was astonished pique that the writers traveling with the Marines in the initial ground offensive *had not been given an opportunity to sleep for two full days!* Of course, the Marines who were doing the fighting were not sleeping either. And a lot more than three servicemen have been killed. But they're from another species.

Typical reporters know little about a fighting life. Many show scant respect for the fighter's virtues. Hardly any could ever be referred to as fighting men themselves. Many of the journalists embedded among U.S. forces that I've crossed paths with are fish out of water here, and show their discomfort clearly as they hide together in the press tents, fantasizing about expensive restaurants at home and plush hotels in Kuwait City, fondling keyboards and satellite phones with pale fingers, clinging to their world of offices and tattle and chatter where they feel less ineffective, less testosterone deficient, more influential.

It's amusing on one level. But reporters are the interpreters for the rest of America of what's real and what's important in the world. And the vast politico-cultural gulf that separates most of them from martial ideals often produces portrayals of military work that are twisted in one fashion or another. Last evening, I listened as a writer for one big city newspaper dripped derision for the soldier's life, squealed about the awfulness of President Bush abandoning U.N. babysitting of Saddam, and sniggered with a TV reporter at attempts to inspire "awe" through a bombing campaign. I almost wished there would be a very loud explosion very nearby just to shut up their rattling. Instead, I walked out into the full-mooned night.

THE REAL ARMY

After weeks of close observation, where I have been granted everything from sensitive information in classified battle briefings to valuable insider tips on how to find a clean privy, I can testify that airborne generals and colonels are not standoffish conference-center commanders. Major General Chuck Swannack informs me he'll be the first one out of an airplane if the brigade does a parachute assault. Lieutenant Colonel Christopher Gehler, who commands the division's attack helicopter battalion, will himself be flying regular combat sorties into potential anti-aircraft fire.

The infantry commander, Colonel Bray, will likewise jump into the thick of battle if it comes to parachute assault, and he's in a particularly aggressive frame of mind these days. The brigade battle briefings he runs are hard as ice, and each ends with all of the roughly fifty officers present jumping to their feet, then flinging themselves to the tent floor where they fly through eighty-two wide-spread push-ups and eighty-two four-rep leg flutters. (As you might expect, eighty-two is a favorite number in this division.)

I run into Bray repeatedly during my time with the 82nd, and the interactions are always interesting. A great hulk of a man, with glistening black skin, large hands, and a racing tongue and mind, Bray has a raw and refreshing bluntness about him. He strikes me as very much a leader rather than a ruler, a vigorous defender of decency and fairness, and an unapologetic killer of tyrannical men.

The evening that I walked out of the press tent in disgust at my fellow journalists, I decided that a quick wash would be just the thing to wipe away the rhetorical smog and physical grit swirling around me. At about midnight I strode into the shower trailer. And who was there washing his socks in a bucket but the commander himself?

I smiled inside, hearing in my mind the criticisms of military "authoritarianism" I've often received from the lips of professors and anchormen. Funny, I don't remember any professor or media celebrity ever washboarding his underwear among his students or studio assistants.

This democratic unpretentiousness pervades our military. Privates and corporals have told me of being grabbed around the neck by General Tommy Franks or some other high commander inquiring how they're doing. And the openness of our military leadership goes much further than this. I've already described the brisk give-and-take I observed between infantry troopers and officers during combat training. In one daily battle update I attended with the brigade leadership, a sharp debate opened up between the chief medical officer and the head chaplain over what sort of risks should reasonably be taken to retrieve the bodies of dead soldiers. There was no sign of sycophancy or intimidated silence in this war council.

Rank is definitely respected in today's U.S. military, but competing ideas are free to contend. In both the physical and intellectual realms, arm wrestling might be thought of as our armed-service model. May the best concept, and biggest bicep, win.

It's not adequately appreciated by American elites how vast a range of individuals serve in our armed forces at present. There are hillbillies and kids from concrete canyons, wealthy suburbanites and first generation immigrants, people with graduate degrees and self-taught mechanical wizards. Consider just a few of the soldiers from the 82nd I've recently become acquainted with:

- A Russian who moved to Brooklyn at age 17, joined up, and now drives the brigade commander.

- A sergeant who had finished most of a Ph.D. in philosophy at Fordham when he decided he'd like to become a paratrooper. That was four years ago.

- A warrant officer who, after breaking into fluent Spanish, explains that he served two years as a religious missionary in Bolivia.

- A bright, self-educated Californian who taught himself German, and is now about halfway through a rigorous Special Forces battlefield medicine course that will leave him qualified to do everything up to and including surgery.

- A chaplain originally from Kenya who grew up so destitute his greatest childhood treat was to sneak sugar from his mother's cupboard.

- A pilot who started in the Army as a mechanic, took a tour as an artilleryman, was selected to fly helicopters, and now has turned himself into an expert on the art of coordinating airstrikes with ground troops, hoping to literally write the book on this subject for the Army.

- A military intelligence officer who, over the last few years, learned first Mandarin and then Arabic at Defense Department language school.

- A lively young medic who turns out to be a graduate of Wesleyan, one of the toniest (and most antimilitary) colleges in the country.

- An amiable Colombian helicopter mechanic who left his home for the United States after guerrillas in that South American nation marked anyone with military helicopter expertise for assassination.

Meshing persons with wildly different backgrounds, educations, personal tastes, and occupational talents is not easy, but the Army does a better job of bridging human gaps than any other large institution I've observed up close. There are far fewer barriers and castes than one finds at a typical civilian corporation, campus, or agency of government. And when this wide spectrum of men turn their minds and bodies to the same task, despotic enemies hardly stand a chance.

As far back as the Civil War, the unusual egalitarianism of the U.S. military was already apparent. "The armies of Europe are machines," wrote General Ulysses Grant in his memoir, "the majority of the soldiers . . . have very little interest in the contest in which they are called to take part." But America's armies are "composed of men who are able to read, men who know what they are fighting for." One aristocratic observer of General William Tecumseh Sherman's army recorded this:

> The officers and men are on terms of perfect equality socially. Off duty they drink together, go arm in arm about the town, call each other by the first name, in a way that startles. . . . A friend heard a private familiarly addressing a brigadier general as "Jake." Miss Lee saw another general taking hold with his men to help move a lot of barrels on a wharf. He took off his coat and worked three hours, like a common porter.

American officers continue to be remarkably grounded and accessible to their troops today. As Colonel Bray twists laundry in his soapy bucket, and I shower and shave, we shoot the breeze about our kids, movies, college, and the like. After brushing our teeth we step out into bright lunar light.

Striding along a dirt path under a full moon, the colonel frets about the security of secret information, and explains to me why he would launch a "very personal, very harsh vendetta" against any journalist who releases advance intelligence that could endanger the lives of his men. As we speak, the ghostly form of two paratroopers approaches us on the road. Suddenly the colonel stops them.

"What are your names?" Replies dart back. "Where are you from?" More replies. Outlines of individual lives began to form. These are two human beings unlike any two others; somebody's son, someone's friend.

Then Bray turns to me. "*They* are why I take this so seriously. Men, carry on."

3

TIME TO FIGHT

THE IDES OF MARCH

MARCH 20—I'm now officially a beneficiary of missile defense. Early this morning, coalition forces got wind from the CIA of a conference of Iraqi leaders that was too tempting to miss. A round of cruise missiles was aimed at the meeting site, inaugurating the first day of America's second Iraq war.

It didn't take long for us to receive a response. About half past noon, the air raid sirens at Camp Champion began to wail. "Dynamite, Dynamite, Dynamite!" exclaimed the loudspeaker (the shorthand for "this is a real attack"), "Scuds inbound from southern Iraq." For a second, all of us in the tent stared at each other wondering if this was just a drill. Then we ripped the Velcro on our gas mask carriers, clapped our masks on, leapt for the bags containing our chemical protective suits, and darted for the Scud bunker.

It became very quiet as we jammed together under the sandbagged concrete culvert. The only sound was the ethereal hissing of the breathing respirators on our masks. Depending on where it's launched from, it would take somewhere between three and thirteen minutes for a ballistic missile to reach us. As the minutes ticked by, the normal Army repartee of jokes, jive, and anti-Saddam oaths slowly returned. "I hope somebody sand-bagged one of the porta-johns," somebody cracked.

Then the loudspeaker began to rumble again. Clearly the announcer was wearing his own gas mask. Despite the muffling, there eventually came this quite intelligible and welcome announcement: "Missile destroyed." Some soldiers told me they heard the explosion of the Patriot thudding on the horizon.

The Patriot system that knocked down these two missiles has been harshly attacked by defense critics for years; more generally, skeptics have savaged the entire concept of missile defense, sneering that the prospect of hitting one missile with another missile is a pipe dream. Well, those of us who spent mid-March in the Kuwaiti desert are here to tell you that ballistic missile defense works, providing civilians and troops alike with a marvelous shield from nasty dangers. If one of Saddam's missiles had landed on a U.S. camp, where military personnel are densely packed in open tents, he could have achieved a psychologically crushing Beirut bombing-style or Khobar Towers–like killing.

Soldiers certainly think highly of the Patriot. "We're gonna have to take those Patriot boys out on the town when we get home," suggested one trooper, with smiling nods all around. Deployed in concentrated camps as they are, they know they're vulnerable, but have learned to trust and love the protective umbrella that the U.S. military now stretches over critical military arenas and nearby cities. The Kuwait camps are reportedly protected by a seven-layer missile defense system.

Just one hour later, the first attack was repeated in almost every particular. Once again a gratifying verdict eventually echoed over the loudspeakers: "Missile destroyed." It became a long day, however, with a total of seven alerts requiring us to throw on our protective gear and pour into the bunkers. As training and meetings and meals had to be canceled, and everyone had to start wearing their full battle rattle all about camp, one could see the very real strains that are put on troops when they face the threat of chem/bio war, even if the attacks are unsuccessful.

Details came out at that evening's briefing among the military leadership. The first Scud launch's plume was detected instantly by the JSTARS airborne battle command center and ground radars. Three Patriot missiles fired in response, obliterating the missile. Almost as quickly, an F-15, A-10, or other attack aircraft was dispatched to annihilate the offending launcher. The second Scud came from further north, above Basra. Two Patriots fired and smashed it down. In these first twenty-four hours we had six confirmed Scud launches: two sailed off in harmless directions, while U.S. anti-missile batteries were a perfect four-for-four in eliminating the ones heading for our military camps.

Inexplicably, media reports failed to properly mark this day as a ringing vindication of missile defense. In addition, the establishment media elided another fundamental lesson of this skirmish: intermediate range ballistic missiles are one of the weapons Saddam Hussein was banned from possessing years ago by U.N. resolution. They are one of the weapons that, just weeks ago, he swore on a stack of Holy Korans he didn't possess. They are one of the weapons U.N. inspectors told us they saw no sign of. They are one of the weapons that Security Council opponents of the United States sniffed that Iraq was now unlikely to possess.

So: On the very first day of hostilities, Saddam revealed himself (once again) to be a liar. Jacques Chirac, Gerhard Schroeder, Nelson Mandela, Kofi Annan, and other apologists for the U.N. inspection charade were shown to be feckless fools. And American anti-ballistic missile technology was demonstrated to be a defensive bulwark of our future.

BATTLE READY

In the Army, sergeants major are the bosses of the factory floor. They are the bridge between enlisted soldiers and commanding officers. And they guide and manage other sergeants—who are the real backbone and institutional memory of the military.

Paul Weidhas—the bluff, sometimes stern, yet kind and good-humored sergeant major of my mates in the helicopter battalion—stops by my cot. Have I got ballistic armor? With supplemental Kevlar hard plates? Let me see your helmet. Got the special canteen that fits with the drinking straw sealed into your gas mask? You need to sew squares of glint tape on your sleeves, your back, and your helmet cover so our soldiers and pilots see you glow in their night sights, recognize you as a friendly, and hold their fire. Do you know your blood type? Write it on your T-shirt. Does somebody have a DNA sample for you? We'll need it if a body part has to be identified.

Before this expedition to the Middle Eastern desert arose so suddenly, I had a plan to go winter camping with a buddy on this very weekend. I expected to ski in with a light pack, toting cocoa and snacks, perhaps risking a late blizzard. Instead, here I was buckled to a gas mask rather than a pair of skis, lugging a decidedly nonlight pack full of batteries, computer, camera, and telecom gear instead of winter woolies, coping with dust storms instead of snow. It occurs to me: When last I used this very backpack, my main worry was smells—my son and I were spending a week in the Wyoming backcountry in the company of grizzlies, to whom you do not want to carry the scent of food, Chap Stick, or chewing gum. Right now, on the other hand, my main concern is color. When you're out in the monotonously brown desert, being the only flash of blue, or green, or red in the region can be a form of begging to get shot at.

As I mulled over these unfamiliar issues, Jake Froehle, the strapping twenty-seven-year-old helicopter pilot and father of two from Alaska who is headquarters company commander, sat a couple of cots away, completing the kind of paperwork that only military officers process: Each of his troopers must fill out a form providing some weirdly intimate personal information that would be used if it became necessary to positively confirm the identity of a shot-down pilot, captured soldier, unknown radio caller, or in some other situation where impersonation is a risk. The written statements are quirky declarations on things like what kind of hair your wife has, or which sibling is your favorite, or some food preference or detail of home life or personal friendship. Jake chuckles perversely, and anonymously shares a few odd details aloud, as he reviews the forms for completeness from his corner of the tent.

All around me the soldiers are getting down to business: Cleaning M-4 carbines and other weapons. Testing radios. Sifting through what should be included in the main battle pack, versus what will go into a second pack which can be abandoned if the soldier gets into deep trouble. I must pack in the same bipartite way. Among the infantry, physical drills have gotten harder, a little savage even.

Throughout the camp, a definite bellicosity is building. These troopers don't want to be left behind as the combat operation builds; they desperately want to carry out the part they've trained so hard for. "All but two of the eighty men in my tent served in Afghanistan last year, and we still had people strangling each other in the competition to get over here. We're ready to fight," forward air controller Buddy McArthur tells me. The missile launches, the odious demands of constant chemical and ballistic protection, the trickling casualty reports, the obnoxious threats continuing to flow from Baghdad, only leave the soldiers around me more testy and itchy for action.

The rhetoric from second-guessers in Europe has also annoyed some. I was in the mess hall when a report aired over the camp TV that French president Jacques Chirac was "warning" the U.S. and Britain against trying to rebuild Iraq without French help. "I'd like to know why France thinks it should have anything at all to say about it," scoffed a sergeant sitting across from me. (Except he said it in French himself—that peculiar English form of French that is spoken by salty paratroopers.) The statement that "Going to war without the French is like going deer hunting without your accordion" got repeated more than once among the troops. As did these: "What do you call a Frenchman advancing on Baghdad? A salesman." And, "How do you know which military rifles among those listed on eBay are French? They're labeled Never been fired. Dropped once."

The brass are nearly as keyed up as the rank and file, but they are proceeding with great patience. They understand the stunning level of destruction their forces could inflict if fully unleashed, and realizing that America will need to fix most of the physical infrastructure it destroys in this war, they are showing great reserve. Force is being ratcheted up only gradually, in hopes that a coup, the death of Saddam, or some other early capitulation by the enemy might spare everyone much unnecessary damage. We are getting lots of military intelligence reporting infighting (even gun battles) within the Iraqi forces, as they hash out their next move.

A good deal of planning and training is going on in camp to prepare our forces to win the peace after the battles end. Civil affairs, intelligence, MP, and psychological operations units are working at crowd control, quick identification of local leaders, aid distribution, and loudspeaker broadcasting in Arabic.

Meanwhile, life goes on. Yesterday was Sunday, and quite possibly the last chapel services before these soldiers go into combat, most of them for the first time. A large tent packed with burly, heavily armed men, their heads bowed intently in prayer, reading from their camouflaged Bibles, and singing out in full throat is quite a sight. The preachers emphasized the importance of individuals getting right with God, and Scripture's many positive references to loyal soldiering in the cause of good.

A number of first-time fathers stood up to announce the birth of their babies this week, reminding us what these men give up to be here. During prayer call at the Protestant services there were requests from sergeants and officers for wisdom so that they might ably lead the soldiers under them. I was struck that several requests for prayers for Iraqis were offered up by servicemen in the congregation—prayers for the safety of Iraqi civilians, and even for Iraqi soldiers, that they might recognize U.S. troops as "liberators not enemies," and not throw their lives away.

This camp is full of a strange mix of no-nonsense ferocity hard amidst deep decency and kindness. That is the noblest, and rarest, mix for any military setting. And it is a characteristically American combination. As far back as the Civil War, American soldiers became famous for waging war fiercely all day, then sharing rations, card games, and water buckets at the same streams with their opponents in the evening. Currently, our Marine Corps is nearly as famous for its "Toys for Tots" program as it is for its high competence with the rifle.

American soldiers wrap goodness and aggressiveness in the very same uniform. When they shoot at people, they rarely miss (as I could soon attest). Yet they don't nurse grudges; they forgive easily; they are gracious, charitable, and humane to opponents. They are the worst people to have as enemies, and the very best to give up to.

TECH VERSUS THE FOG OF WAR

The early sprint through southern Iraq by U.S. Marines and the Army's 3rd Infantry Division was a welcome kickoff to the war. Relatively few lives were lost, and the key southern oilfields and ports were secured mostly undamaged. Yet the speed of the southern rollup was no great surprise. Iraq's south has long been a kind of rebel province due to religious and cultural schisms separating it from Baghdad.

Days and even weeks before any hostilities commenced, certain Iraqi troops and border guards were trying to surrender to U.S. troops across the Kuwaiti fence. Noting that no war was yet underway, the Americans sent them back. "I guess we can think of these guys as pre-positioned POWs," stated one military intelligence officer with a straight face at a nightly pre-war battle briefing.

The 82nd's commander, General Swannack, has granted the embedded journalists unusual access to his councils of war. I've attended a number of so-called BUBs (battle update briefs)—at the division, brigade, and battalion levels. These are the central daily events for sharing intelligence and planning missions, and have always previously been closed to any but officers with secret clearances. I'm told that only a handful of journalists in the war theater were accorded this privilege during the combat planning phases.

To give us a sense of how a battle is controlled, Karl Horst, the bright, personable, thick-necked, multilingual colonel who is the division chief of staff (making him General Swannack's top assistant here) gives me and four or five other reporters a tour of their new Digital Command Center. Two years ago, battles were still run using paper maps, pins, Post-it notes, and overhead projectors. Today, a complex of up to seventeen separate computer information screens is projected on a large wall, under three clocks set to relevant time zones, surrounded by rings of tables crowned with laptops where perhaps forty officers monitor individual components of communication and data.

The main battle screen is a map, upon which critical boundaries are imposed—artillery ranges, air defense zones, political limits. A brand new Northrop Grumman system known as "Blue Force Tracker" allows commanders to see the true, exact location of all friendly forces with no delay from lagging radio or courier reports. Vehicles of all sorts—trucks, tanks, ships, airplanes—have been fitted with transceivers that constantly send their GPS coordinates back to headquarters. Intelligence reports on enemy positions are layered on top of this to create a composite battle map.

Soldiers in the field can also send back information

on minefield locations, downed bridges, chemically contaminated areas, and such. These get entered onto the central battlefield map, which is in turn shared digitally by all units out in the field. The system will even automatically set off an alarm in a vehicle whenever it wanders dangerously close to an enemy position, mines, or some other hazard the field commander might not have noticed.

Both HQ and individual units out in the battle zone can thus easily monitor the relative positions of friendly armor, artillery, and supply units; the progress of ships carrying critical supplies; the nearness of the enemy; and so forth. A similar screen portrays the exact location, type, and direction of all aircraft in the sky. (Good guys show up as green, bad planes are red.) Someday it will become practical to extend elements of this tracking system right down to the level of the individual soldier. Live or taped video feeds from helicopters, Predator drones, or surveillance planes can also be fed onto the battle center screens.

None of this is foolproof. Friendly fire accidents and the like will never be completely eliminated. But great progress has been made.

One panel is an index page for the division's Web site, which is where all information is now disseminated. Until quite recently, any sensitive new order used to be typed, photocopied, then dispatched by courier to as many as fifty different subcommand nodes. Today, new orders are simply posted on SIPRNET, the encrypted military intranet, where all commanders can have instant access to them, as well as voluminous archived background information.

The interestingly named Major Miner, who has put much of this hardware together, reports that the system is made to be broken down and rebuilt quickly. Within eight hours of when the first parachute pops in an airborne assault, this entire command center can be set up afresh in the middle of the battlefield. With its own power, and coded satellite links to the entire globe, commanders will be able to see and assess almost any aspect of their fight, as well as the larger war.

"I want you to go out and look your paratroopers in the eye," stated General Swannack as he closed one division BUB. "I want you to make sure they're ready. Because this fight, like all fights, will ultimately be won by our infantrymen and sergeants." Which is certainly true.

But today more than ever before, the men moving the chess pieces inside the battle centers can also make a tide turn. They now have current, accurate information that can make all the difference between success and failure, life and death. The fog of war will never be blown away altogether; but it's thinning.

PRESSURE BUILDS, THEN BREAKS

Some advance elements of the 82nd Airborne, mostly supply units, have already trickled north into Iraq, following the armored elements that plowed open the road. Out in our camp's staging area, almost all of the division's vehicles are now fully loaded, their tarps pulled tight. The frantic calculations of the loadmasters responsible for fitting into a limited number of airplanes everything the assault force will need to fight a battle for several days are nearly finished. We're ticking close to our D day.

I ask Captain Andy Reiter, a quiet, pleasant twenty-seven-year-old Kiowa pilot who grew up solid in a Wyoming mining town, then went to West Point, how he feels about the prospect of flying his small helicopter into real anti-aircraft fire for the first time. He looks at me soberly, steadily, with piercing blue eyes. He knows how to respond to various threats—never flying the same route twice, turning his turbine's exhaust port away from a heat-seeking missile in a last-second dart, other forms of evasion. The threat that worries him most, he says, is a rocket-propelled grenade blasted straight up from the ground as he buzzes in low. There's really no preparing for that.

Because of the media embedding that has made this an almost instant-broadcast war, the soldiers have gotten a close-up glimpse of what could lie ahead for them. Many were angry and riled when news arrived that Americans captured by the Iraqis had been abused and executed. Some said it was time to change the name of the effort from Operation Iraqi Freedom to Operation Iraqi Asswhuppin'.

Our military leaders had been expecting skullduggery. One intelligence briefing I observed warned that certain Iraqi military groups had purchased American-style uniforms, and that they aimed to commit atrocities against Iraqi citizens in these which they hoped would be blamed on coalition forces. But now the dirty tricks cascaded in some unexpected ways.

Everyone seemed surprised that there were false surrenders. A large number of Marines were wounded and killed when Iraqis waving the white flag suddenly pulled hidden weapons and attacked the Americans accepting their capitulation. Another group of Marines was forced to halt a firefight when the Special Republican Guard unit they were battling dragged a number of women and children into their front lines. The Americans pulled back, unsure how to proceed. In other places, Baath party irregulars shed their uniforms and began to fight in civilian clothes. Of course, the people most endangered by these dishonorable actions were everyday Iraqis, whom American troops were now forced to treat as risks, rather than people needing help.

No matter how graphic the TV footage in the mess hall, however, the troops never get grim. There is a surprising amount of music in the camp—with numerous soldiers having brought guitars, and showing that they know how to use them. Some breathtakingly good singing takes place at chapel services, and in impromptu evening jam sessions in the tents.

This afternoon, as I sat writing from some notes

spread across my cot, a clutch of black and white soldiers clustered ten feet away, kicking back in our shady tent on this hot day, reminiscing warmly about favorite odd foods cooked by their mothers and grandmothers: pigs feet, pickled cabbage, apple butter, red hot dogs, chitterlings, fried cornbread, mountain oysters (bull testicles), boudin (Creole rice-and-blood sausage). "My granddaddy used to give me whiskey, honey, and a piece of peppermint mixed in a glass when I was sick," smiled one sergeant. "Man, we used to pretend something was achin' just to get some of that."

UP THE EUPHRATES

4

IN IRAQ

BRAND NEW GAME PLAN

MARCH 25—The camp was aflutter all night, and today we learned the 82nd is going into action. General Swannack offered a briefing on the division's fresh orders at 0830 Zulu time. (Zulu, or "Z," hours refer to Greenwich mean time, the global standard which the military uses for operations to avoid confusion as orders cross time zones.) The division had been assigned an entirely new mission. Instead of seizing Baghdad International Airport by parachute assault—the 82nd's long-planned assignment as part of the move on Iraq's capital city—the men were now charged to take up their other specialty: urban warfare.

As the Army's 3rd Infantry Division and the 1st Marine Expeditionary Force raced up Highway 8 toward Baghdad, they largely bypassed the cities along the route. After being ringed by coalition forces, Basra, Iraq's second largest metropolis, quickly erupted in street fighting between Iraqis revolting against Saddam Hussein and hardcore defenders of the regime. British forces were given the task of stabilizing that city.

The next town up the highway, Nasiriyah, has been the scene of some of the sharpest fighting in the south, including all the dirty tricks of false surrenders, fighting in civilian clothing, using innocents as shields. It too was sealed off for door-to-door cleanup, this to be done by the Marines.

At this writing, the third city up the Euphrates, Samawah, is likewise being used as a hiding ground for hardcore Baath party fighters and fedayeen partisans. They are carrying out terrorism across the city, and guerrilla warfare in the countryside—including ambushing the U.S. supply convoys that pass by on their way toward Baghdad. After engaging, these fighters melt back into the streets of the 180,000-person urban area. The 82nd has been ordered to clean these irregulars out of the city.

And so, within a span of hours, the entire brigade has had to shift its plans from a parachute assault to an infantry sweep. Many of the troopers will drive the 240 miles to Samawah in armed convoy. The rest will fly up in transport planes. I'll go by land, hoping to get a closer look at the terrain and battle sites along the way. We're told there has been a lot of shooting on this road.

Each of the soldiers has drawn 210 rounds for his M-4 or M-16, 45 rounds for his 9mm pistol, and more than 800 cartridges for the machine gunners. Lieutenant Colonel Gehler climbs onto the back of a Humvee and gives a stern speech telling the troops to put on a combat mentality, to choose action over inaction, to be aggressive as soon as we cross the berm into Iraq. This route we'll be driving is where the heaviest action of the war has taken place, and it needn't be an enemy tank to be a threat—attacks are being made from schoolbuses and taxis, by people who look like civilians.

The colonel assures all that their rules of engagement allow unencumbered self-defense against any apparent threat. No radioing for permission to shoot. No more asking for orders.

If the convoy is attacked, the escorted vehicles will keep rolling at all costs. But the seventy members of Alpha Troop, cavalry assigned to provide the helicopter battalion with security, will pull over and engage the enemy with the Mark 19 grenade launchers, .50 caliber machine guns, TOW missile launchers, and M-240 machine guns mounted on the roofs of their Humvees, plus the rifles they carry. I'm riding in one of these gun trucks with three Alpha troopers: Private O'Connor, Sergeant Campos, and Lieutenant Mosby.

When the division's various elements regroup closer to Samawah, new base camps will be established from which daily missions can be run into the city and outlying lairs. Saddam's guerrillas will be tracked down and eliminated. It promises to be delicate and dangerous work.

OVER THE BORDER

It's an eerie feeling rolling down a crowded highway at up to forty miles per hour, with all the vehicle lights taped over, in total darkness. Everyone except me is wearing night-vision goggles (which infantrymen call NODs; pilots prefer the term NVGs). Even goggled up, though, driving in blackout is dangerous. Several hours into our trip, a Kuwaiti truck on a dirt road crossing our highway, itself driving with no lights, piles into the side of one of the darkened Humvees, injuring two soldiers and sending the driver of the pickup through the windshield.

Taking part in a convoy like this makes you realize how much of the Army is just a giant trucking operation. Supply, supply, supply. Literally hundreds of cargo carriers of all descriptions roar down the road, humping troopers, fuel, water, food, rucksacks, generators, medical supplies, ammo, you name it.

Keeping this massive string of overstuffed vehicles together in a secure formation is an exercise in hurry up and wait. There is a kind of science to secure convoying, and because of what is known as the "slinky effect," the limiting factor is the acceleration speed of the slowest freighter in the line. Thus, much of the night we rumble along at about thirty miles per hour or less. There are numerous stops for breakdowns, refueling, lost drivers, and the like.

Between the herky-jerky movement, the heavy stink of diesel, the rattle of loose sheet metal, the hissing radio, and the lumpy armor and chem suits we're wearing inside the cramped Humvees (seemingly designed for lower-body amputees), it's a blue-ribbon recipe for cabin fever and deep vein thrombosis. But we're all a little keyed up and tolerate the physical displeasure surprisingly easily.

At 0103 we cross a breach in the fence and enter Iraq. The road is lined with burned-out buildings and vehicle hulks from the last Gulf War. But a shot-up armored personnel carrier and security truck are more recent relics of this week's fight. A dead man sits in the truck, his windshield perforated, his mouth open, his door swinging—an advertisement for tardy escape reflexes. Off in the distance, a large fire burns a hole in the horizon.

We're running up the infamous Highway of Death, where the rats fleeing Kuwait in 1991, their vehicles stuffed with plunder, were strafed and bombed into eternity by coalition pilots. Even in the inkiness of night, a series of vehicle graveyards shine alongside the road. As we edge closer to dawn, the sky becomes crystalline for the first time since I've been in the dust-swirled Middle

East; a warmly familiar set of stars crowns our heads, even as the ground beneath our feet and wheels becomes ever more strange.

At 0630, the lieutenant is driving, and after a long night of navigating and surfing the radio traffic he is falling asleep. Whenever he starts to swerve off the highway either the gunner (who, with his head sticking out of the top of the jeep, is wide awake in the cold air) or I, sitting behind the driver's seat, whack the lieutenant to waken him. We do this over and over. After we stop, we hear that an identical drill was taking place in nearly all the vehicles, giving new meaning to the phrase "back seat driver."

Nearly twenty-two hours after our start, we pull off the highway and onto a narrow track. In the distance I notice what looks like . . . could it possibly be the Ziggurat of Ur? I pull out my binoculars and, sure enough, I'm thrilled to take in the instantly recognizable four thousand-year-old Sumerian temple constructed by the world's very first civilized humans. The civility of more recent residents is open to question. What kind of barbarian would build a massive concrete and steel military base right next to one of the three or four oldest human structures in the world?

For, turning onto a dirt road, we immediately enter one of Saddam Hussein's biggest air bases. Here, the 82nd will establish a forward camp. At the base entrance, there are two of the obligatory large portraits of the maximum leader. Next to the main one, some GI with a sense of humor has erected a cardboard sign. It reads: Bush International Airport.

HOME AWAY FROM HOME

TALLIL AIR BASE, SOUTH-CENTRAL IRAQ, MARCH 26—We eat our first food in nearly a day, MRE pot luck, inside one of the twenty or thirty ruined concrete bunkers where Saddam used to hide his MiGs. The bunkers are impressive in scale, but a close look shows the concrete work to be painfully shoddy. And the charred jet and helicopter hulks in the yards outside testify to the insufficiency of Iraq's crude fortifying instincts.

This is Tallil Air Base, which used to be one of Iraq's strongholds. It was pounded by U.S bombers in the first Gulf War—some of the six-foot-thick concrete hangar walls have been neatly perforated by bunker-buster bombs—and the whole facility has taken on an air of wrack and ruin, which is not surprising given that Iraq's air force nearly ceased to exist a dozen years ago. This was still an active military facility a week ago, however, until the Army's 3rd Infantry Division swept through and cleaned it out.

After it is cleared of bombs and debris, we'll set up a semi-permanent post in one of the abandoned bunkers. Tonight we're sleeping under the stars on a concrete apron. Determined to pack light I left my camping mat home, so tomorrow I'll be the guy with the flat spot on the back of his head.

We are on a sprawling plain with unsecured boundaries, and vulnerable to attack should there be any dead-enders in the area. Defensive preparations begin with the same action as in prairie schooner days: The wagons are circled in a tight loop around the mouth of the bunker. Patrols wearing NODs will watch our perimeter all night; they chamber cartridges as they move out. If nature calls, don't go out far or you could be mistaken for a hajji.

Sergeant Major Weidhas is really taking care of me, as he does his soldiers. He suggests it would be a good idea for me to know how to use the sidearms that serve as a second weapon within the 82nd's ranks. He walks me through a quick tutorial on loading and firing the Army Beretta. He promises a primer on the standard M-4 carbine next.

Major Jim Corcoran, the regiment's helpful executive officer, has just briefed me on the latest details of our mission. U.S. mechanized units have the bottom crescent of Samawah sealed off. The 82nd will start in the east and sweep across the middle and top of the city. No one knows exactly what lies ahead, but a CIA agent inside the gates radioed in a whispered report during the night that members of the Fedayeen Saddam are holed up and preparing to defend the metropolis. Exploratory helicopter and infantry patrols will start tonight or tomorrow.

If the next city over is any model for what to expect in Samawah, there may be a hot reception. The Marines went into Nasiriyah yesterday and took forty casualties in stiff street fighting. Dirty tricks continue. I am told it's been determined that the American soldiers taken prisoner and then executed in the early days of the war were caught by using children to lure them close to some camouflaged ditches where fighters lay in ambush.

STARTING WITH A BANG

The men are in great spirits tonight, and ready for action. They're sober enough, though. Around sunset, a massive fireball erupts down the plain, followed by a mushroom cloud, and last a huge boom. The radio reports that an Army EOD (Explosive Ordnance Division) team exploded a large cache of mortars uncovered at the edge of the base. Irregulars had mortar tubes all set up, and rounds stockpiled, to unload on American positions under cover of darkness.

One powerfully built young officer confided shortly after the shock wave passed that the spectacular flames and noise were a reminder for him that military work is all about destruction and loud jolts and other scary things. These men aren't insensitive to the dangers around them, they just proceed in spite of them.

One of the squad commanders walks around to each of his helo pilots, one at a time, puts his face next to theirs, and asks if they're ready to fly tonight if the general calls. Are they rested enough to handle the trickiness of NVG-navigating for several hours? Are they mentally ready to get fired at? Colonel Gehler is lobbying hard for a decent night's sleep before his pilots enter the fray, but the infantry officers in the 325th are reportedly gung ho to start whacking at the hornet's nest right away.

A friendly and handsome blond-haired pilot named Jeff Sumner invites me to use his camping stove to make some tea. We talk about our families. He was set to marry this month until the Middle East called. He says his fiancee, a pharmacist in Shreveport, Louisiana, was understanding. When interrogated about his flightworthiness Jeff somberly tells his leader he's tired but thinks he could do three or four hours under goggles if there's an emergency. Even if no helicopter mission is scheduled, a 911 call is always possible should some infantry unit get pinned down.

At the medevac facility being set up here at Tallil, we saw wounded soldiers and Marines being brought in this afternoon. On the drive back across the base, Major Corcoran reports, there were dead bodies, tags on their toes, waiting in the same area.

At about 0400 a soldier in full battle gear taps me in my sleeping bag. "Reynolds?"

"No, next man over."

"Reynolds, it's your turn for guard duty."

As I come to, I notice that not far off in the distance some helicopters are winding up. One takes off. Then another. I'm wondering who is behind the controls, and where they're going.

I look up at the sparkling sky. Then, with a lower glance, my brain takes in the bunker, the trucks, the outline of a rifle nearby. Still the same familiar stars. Still the same decidedly unhomelike land they're shining down upon.

MEAT AND POTATOES

I'm enjoying a split life: part of my day with the suave, tightly wound pilots, part with the earthier, more ribald cavalry troopers who provide the unit's ground security. A perfect meat and potatoes combination for warfighting, and also for story collecting.

As I sat on the ground yesterday eating from a plastic pouch, two cavalry buddies being tormented by the swarming flies had an extended time-passing conversation on the cosmic justification for pests.

"What the hell use are flies? I'd like to know one good thing they do for the world."

"Dude, you're thinking small. I saw it on the Discovery Channel: Flies lay their eggs on trash and crap, and the maggots eat it all up."

"Hey, you could put a bucket of maggots on each of the craps we produced here today and there'd still be crap left behind when they're done."

"But not as much. Definitely less crap."

"Yeah, and then there's mosquitos. And fleas. And chiggers. I think there should be just one global, universal pest for all purposes. Fewer options out there to bother us."

"Man, you're such a white suburbanite! Thinking too much, all the time."

"All right, then you tell me the reason for jellyfish. I am quite certain there is no good purpose for jellyfish. I mean . . ."

Cavalry are pretty much what the name implies—fast moving scouts and raiders who literally live on their mounts. Unlike the rest of the Army around them, they pitch no tents. They sleep on the hood, in the back, and across the horribly cramped seats of their Humvees, nap in the shade underneath the trucks by day (because their most important guarding is often done at night), and remain always ready to roll on a moment's notice. Cavalry charge in to save more lightly armed soldiers when they get trapped or ambushed, protect command posts and supply lines, and swoop down to destroy enemy vehicles (including even tanks) in packs. The personalities of the troopers tend to be as slashing and devil-may-care as their duties.

And this is their moment. For helicopter pilots there are lots of thrills even in peacetime. For airborne infantry, jumping out of planes and fighting hand to hand in bullpens can be almost as challenging during training as in the real thing. But for cavalry troopers, it's almost impossible to re-create within a training exercise the free-floating, slash-and-burn buccaneering that combat brings.

Recovering from our twenty-two-hour roadtrip, we are enjoying a lazy morning. Someone has built a fire to burn garbage, and the happy simpleton we'll call Ricky, who is a kind of mascot for the rest of Alpha Troop, is dancing around, exulting for hours over the pops he finds he can make by throwing empty water bottles into the flames with their caps on. Ricky is sweet-tempered, hardworking, and very slow-witted—and beloved by the other cavalrymen. Recounting Ricky stories is a favorite pastime among them.

Ricky is a driver, and this morning his sergeant is hilariously and quite profanely describing one of his latest foibles. It seems Ricky's determination to stick rigidly to the agreed speed limits during our convoy had him staring down, bent necked, at the speedometer most of the night—to the point where he kept veering off the road. All night long it was "Watch out Ricky, you're on the shoulder!" "Get your damn eyes off the needle Ricky!" "What the hell good does it do to go the right speed, Rickster, if you're in the bushes?" and "Ricky, I'm not gonna yell if you go twenty-four instead of twenty-five, but I'm gonna kill you if you drive into that ditch!"

Sergeant Campos and Private O'Connor add a little firepower to our ride, digging out of its case an AT4 rocket (a kind of point-and-shoot disposable bazooka) to add to the Humvee's rooftop armory. Lieutenant Mosby takes a few moments to synchronize the truck's plugger (GPS device) with his handheld unit.

Out here with the cav, I'm observing the *field* end of the Blue Force Tracker in action. Mosby was a computer science major at West Point and he's taken to the new toy with enthusiasm, tutoring some of the more electronics-averse sergeants around him on its fine points. Whereas a few months ago he would have perched in the front passenger seat with a paper map on his lap, he now has not only much better digital maps on an electronic screen, but also a valuable source of what soldiers call "situational awareness." He has, for instance, just been looking up where the infantry elements of our task force were located last night.

BURIED NUTS AND WARTHOGS

TALLIL, MARCH 27—We uncovered a little surprise this morning. I had just sat down for a breakfast of chicken and salsa (in the land of MREs, every meal is dinner) when some older guys decided that what looked like a buried wheel and hubcap, located maybe eight feet from me, was possibly an antitank mine. A Humvee was parked just short of it, and the guys had been stumbling over it all night in the dark on their way out to pee. This morning, Cory O'Connor, who was in high school in

Rhode Island ten months ago, actually jumped up and down on top of it. Curiosity, I guess.

Luckily, tank mines, unlike the antipersonnel versions, take thousands of pounds of pressure to detonate. Just the same, I pick a new breakfasting spot a little further back. Wouldn't want to get any dirt and rocks in my salsa.

After finishing the vegetable cracker with peanut butter and the poundcake (I'd rate it about seven on a sixteen ounce scale), I walk over to look at a giant stinging centipede one guy has cornered. Turns out he (the trooper, not the centipede) was in this exact location back in '91.

"There were about fifty tanks in this air base that we had to take out. The 82nd Airborne had Sheridan armored vehicles back then, and I was in one. Almost met my maker here, actually, at the hand of some Iraqis hiding behind a berm. But between aerial bombs and our TOW missiles and A-10s we finally killed the tanks off. Then we destroyed all the aircraft here. After we ran out of rounds to blast them with we started running over the Hind and Hip helicopters with our Sheridan."

Sergeant Cory Kroll—perfectly described to me as having an exterior as gruff as a Montana grizzly bear enfolding the persona of a kindly father of four girls—tells a similar story. He entered Tallil after Air Force planes and Army attack helicopters had softened things up, but still took heavy fire. "I was the gunner in an armored personnel carrier and we killed a T-55 tank and a bunker. But there were some close calls. An Iraqi jumped up from a camouflaged position and fired an RPG that whistled right between the turrets of my vehicle and the one next to me."

The Air Force must be gaining confidence in the security of the Tallil airfield, because a squadron of A-10 Thunderbolts has just been moved in here to support the infantry operations to the north. Popularly known as the Warthog, the A-10 is a legendary plane, unslick in every regard, but beloved of any American military man who has ever put boot to earth with a rifle on his back.

Even an Air Force ground controller like Buddy McArthur, who makes his living calling in close airstrikes from B-52s, F-15s, B-1s and other needle-nosed craft toting cool laser-guided munitions, says his favorite tool for sheer effectiveness is the A-10. The troopers who've maneuvered with A-10s swear the plane noticeably slows whenever it fires its massive six-barrel 30mm cannon. In fact, they claim that's why the gun was mounted offset on the fuselage—because early models where it was mounted parallel actually stalled in the air during heavy firing. In any case, the plane has a mighty unhealthful effect on enemy tanks and infantry.

But this is a war where good weapons are only one part of the solution. Captain Robin Brown just stopped by with the latest news. She's the battalion's efficient, spirited operations officer. (She and her husband are both helicopter pilots; he's currently vacationing in Afghanistan while she entertains herself further south.) She reports that a minivan roared through an Army checkpoint just north of here and exploded a suicide bomb, killing five soldiers.

Overall, though, the night's momentum flowed strongly in the other direction. Hot off the C-130s that brought them north from Camp Champion, infantrymen from the 82nd's 1st Battalion of the 325th Regiment trucked up to the fringes of Samawah, disembarked, and maneuvered on foot up to a ditch and berm some Iraqi fighters had dug along a major pipeline. They killed seventeen opposing fighters during the night, while sustaining no casualties of their own, and took numerous prisoners of war, who are now corralled behind some wire just down the road from where I sit. If I had to guess, Colonel Bray was right there along the berm himself much of the night.

UP IN THE AIR

During our first eerie night at Tallil, before any helicopter sorties had been run, there was a distinct, understandable edginess in the pilots' tents. But the next day, having flown a few missions without encountering any especially nasty anti-aircraft fire, the old surety and humor came back. Show me a cocky pilot and I'll show you a happy pilot.

The infantry pushing into Samawah from the east were taking mortars in addition to rifle fire, and the Kiowas went up repeatedly to add extra firepower. Lieutenant Sosa fired a Hellfire missile into a building which was being used as a site to rain shells down on the 325th. Mortar silenced, eight guerrillas dead. Just now, the radio has crackled news that pilots Kirschbaum and Marx rocketed a motorcycle that had been spraying AK-47 fire as it raced down a street.

A little earlier, Charlie Company commander Jack Murphy, a fun-loving pilot with a stock of stories about Canadian girlfriends from his years at Fort Drum in northern New York, encountered a hostile crowd of about 40 irregulars in an open area. They began firing AK-47s at his Kiowa. He responded by launching a shrapnel-filled fléchette rocket, ending that threat.

The Kiowas were returning with their missile racks empty after each sortie, then cycling back out to lay more Hellfires and rockets on paramilitaries and the buildings from which they were firing. Our pilots were getting as well as giving. Kirschbaum and Marx returned from one flight with six bullet holes through the underbelly of their bird. Surprisingly, given the light build of the Kiowa, there were no injuries and the helicopter remained flyable. "The shots missed the fuel tank. And fortunately they passed through a narrow six inch strip that's directly between two sensitive areas which, if hit, would almost certainly have ignited an electrical fire," Murphy tells me.

In addition, landings after dark turned out to be dangerous, because the powdery dust kicked up on descent hides the ground even in night-vision goggles. There were some hard touchdowns before the decision was made to suspend blackout operations, perhaps until some Rhino Snot (a kind of plasticizer) can be sprayed on the sand and dust to seal a landing surface. Of course the on-call Quick Reaction Force is an exception; if there are soldiers in danger, they'll fly despite the risk.

Overall, it's been a solid stretch for the aviation regiment. Captain Brown is ebullient when I run into her: "We were kicking ass today."

5

CLOSER TO THE FRONT

PLANS CHANGE

THE IRAQI DESERT SOUTH OF SAMAWAH, MARCH 28—If you can't roll with a punch and adapt to entirely new circumstances within a fingersnap, you don't belong in warfighting. Just now it's been decided that, less than twenty-four hours after settling into their abandoned bunker, the battalion needs to have a base closer to Samawah. Tallil is still about forty-five minutes flying time from the main battle zone, and by the time the Kiowas get there and back, and leave themselves a small fuel cushion, they only have enough gas for thirty to forty-five minutes of fighting time.

So a skeleton crew will pull up stakes and set up a small command center and good sized FARP (forward arming and refueling point) much closer to Samawah. That'll give the helicopters a place to quickly pick up more ammo and fuel before they hop back into the fray inside the city. I decide to follow the action north. My friends in the Alpha Troop cavalry are being dispatched to provide security for this new base, which will start as little more than a few tents and a sprawling jet fuel bladder or string of tankers in the dust alongside the road. I squeeze into a gun truck with Sergeant Cory Kroll, Specialist Josh Farley, and Private Chad Stapp.

On the drive up, the radio buzzes with reports of frenetic action by the Kiowa pilots, and I'm suddenly wondering if I should have stayed back at the main air base where I could debrief the pilots as they came off shift. When I discover that the future FARP is a hellhole of Iraqi hellholes—a wasteland of shoe-deep dust without so much as a blade of living growth—I again second-guess my judgment in drifting out here. I wouldn't lay down to sleep in this red-brown talcum powder, full of scorpions and stinging centipedes, if the alternative was to stand all night.

The only domicile in sight for miles on this flat, tree-less plain, is a 15' × 15' tent—which turns out to be the brand new world headquarters of the 82nd Airborne Division. Unbeknownst to me, the commanding general also wanted to get closer to the action than Tallil allowed, so he has relocated his command center to the site of the FARP-to-be. Talk about direct access to the brass: Suddenly I'm part of the inner circle whether anyone wants me there or not.

Literally the only objects in this dust bowl aside from the dust are three large tanker trucks laden with jet fuel (the downpayment on a helo gas station), six gun trucks, and the lonely command tent with a handful of Humvees parked next to it. Inside the canvas flaps of the CG's temporary battle center are the top officers running the division. Alpha Troop's gun trucks positioned in a ring around them provide a total of about twenty men, fifteen truck-mounted weapons, and some of the best thermal night sights possessed by the U.S. Army.

And that is literally all that blocks General Swannack and his brain trust (as well as the rest of us) from becoming casualties or prisoners of war in an enemy hot zone. All day long this immediate area has seen mortar firings, artillery strikes, and paramilitary infiltrations. Very nearby, a Bradley came over a berm and stumbled upon a group of Iraqi irregulars, blasting them into oblivion. The 325th's foot soldiers are now sweeping through Samawah proper, routing enemy positions and racking up double-digit kills every day. Yet in a ring all around us, the magical optics reveal, the desert still crawls with suspicious men.

ON HAIR TRIGGER

As the night deepens, F-16s thud five-hundred-pound bombs onto buildings just north of us, then circle back above our heads to *boom, boom, boom* a second and third and fourth and fifth time. Later, we watch an American M-1 pound out several rounds at some other target. Meanwhile, the gunner manning the TOW missile launcher on the roof of our Humvee, southern Californian Josh Farley, is finding a regular ant farm of activity out in the darkness between us and Samawah.

This crew values the optical sight of the TOW at least as much as the weapon itself. If we get close enough to a tank to need a TOW somebody hasn't done his job. But the imaging system—a quarter-million dollars worth of glass and electronics—is an invaluable tool for surveilling one's day and night surroundings at up to several miles away. "We can see a guy smoking a cigarette miles out. At a half mile we can see facial expressions and if they have weapons," reports Sergeant Kroll.

"Sergeant, I see a black SUV. Looks almost like a small bus. Now it's meeting up with a pickup truck. Several men are getting out," says Farley.

"Range?"

"Lasing now. Two-two-zero-five meters."

"Any weapons visible?"

"I can't quite see."

"I want you to track them tightly, Farley, you hear?"

"I've also got four dismounted individuals climbing up on some buildings. I was watching those buildings in daylight, Sergeant, and they were empty. Now they're climbing up on the roof of the buildings. They're out at five-one-five-three meters."

"What are they doing?"

"The ones on the ground seem to be handing something up to the ones on the roof. I can confirm that now; they're handing up boxes."

"Weapons?"

"They're too far to tell."

"That's beyond TOW range, Farley. Our max shot is around thirty-seven fifty meters. Give me a grid and I'll call those dudes in to Gillespie's mortar crew."

"Three-six-five/five-nine-three."

"Meantime we'll get on the radio to see if there might be any friendlies out in those sectors. I'll bet the farm those are bad dudes, the way they're acting. But they could just be Bedouins stashing MREs. They were picking them up along the convoy route and taking them out of broken-down transport trucks all day long.

"And there *are* some Special Forces who operate in this area out of SUVs and other nontactical vehicles. That's how you can get fratricide if you're not careful. So just keep watching them Farley. We'll ask our Air Force controllers to have somebody fly over them and see if they can tell anything more about what they're doing.

"Now you go back to that SUV and pickup, Farley. Don't lose them."

"They're parking behind a dirt ridge, about four feet high. But I can still see their hoods over the top. Actually, now the pickup is gone. Damn. Let me look for it."

"Don't worry about those dirt berms. Your TOW missile will rip right through them. You know that, right?"

"Roger. All right, I got the pickup again. It's moving. Toward us. Fast. It's running behind a little levee, roughly southwest. Range now nineteen hundred meters."

"If you see any pink tracers I want you to light up that vehicle, Farley, you got that? Right now, right quick."

"Roger. Range now eighteen fifteen."

"Don't nobody stand behind that missile tube for about seventy feet, or you'll get toasted. And Karl, be ready for a badass noise."

And so for about forty-five strained minutes we were on the brink of launching a missile and mortar strike. Eventually, the action out in the dark subsided. These may be Iraqi irregulars up to no good. But following the general pattern of this war it's decided to wait for them to reveal themselves as a definite threat rather than take the risk of hitting some Bedouins or friendlies. Farley and co-gunner Chad Stapp carefully track the quadrant in front of us all night, ready to pull a trigger on a moment's notice if a weapon is spotted, occasionally getting a start when a desert hare leaps across their lens.

The individuals out there in the gloam could never guess they are being so closely watched from far away. They have no clue they're being repeatedly illuminated, because the laser on the TOW is invisible to the naked eye. Sometimes Farley will point out to an adjoining gun truck a person in need of watching by painting him with his laser while the other cavalryman observes through a night-vision lens. "Man, I'm gonna give this guy cancer from lasing him so much," Farley jokes.

The trucks thirty yards to our north and one hundred yards south represent the final outposts of local civilization, with miles and miles of hostile territory stretching to the horizon in all directions. In total blackness, these few American soldiers hunt predators who are hunting us. Our lives depend on the competence and stamina of the men at the scopes.

By now, the F-16 bomb drops and the tank firing have ceased. The paramilitaries of Samawah took a hard beating from the 82nd Airborne today, but tomorrow will be another day. The radio traffic in our Hummer reveals that the general staff hidden behind blackout canvas a stone's throw away is planning a feint tomorrow morning, aiming to draw the Republican Guard and supporting militias out from their holes. It's been an exhausting, tense evening.

And I'm extremely glad I didn't stay back at Tallil to

interview pilots, or spend the night over at the general's battle tent. For I've just witnessed several vivid hours of ground-level warfighting, in which a grizzled veteran sergeant and a sharp-eyed young soldier uncovered, sorted, and dispatched a range of threats. It is reliable execution of this kind of basic soldiering, repeated over and over by thousands of individuals in hundreds of places, that makes our Army so formidable.

As I type this it is the middle of the night, and I'm being swept by a wave of fatigue. I'm not expecting any more than a few restless hours of sleep snatched upright in a rough truck seat, but even that suddenly seems a great luxury. For no sleep at all—and conceivably not even another sweet day of life—would accrue to me or the other individuals in this circle of trucks if it wasn't for a handful of tough men willing to force themselves awake all night: Scanning, studying, aligning cross hairs on threats, watching to make sure no armed killers crawl into our laps. They are literally the only reason that I (and, at longer range, you and the rest of America) can drift off peacefully when slumber beckons.

Thanks, guys.

SHEET METAL MATTRESS

A sheet metal mattress, a Kevlar pillow, a warm groaning engine beneath me, and a 105-millimeter long-range alarm clock. Put it together and it yields my fondest sleep in two weeks.

Kroll and Stapp curled up in their front seats, and Farley flitted between his rooftop gun nest and a poncho spread on the ground next to the truck. So I unrolled my sleeping bag on the hood of the Humvee, my helmet wedged on the airlift hook to prevent me from rolling down the slope and off the nose. Every couple of hours the team would start up the Humvee to recharge the batteries of the large computer that runs the TOW sight and aiming mechanism. Which turned out to be pure pleasure. The diesel underneath me sent a very wifelike warmth rippling through my bag—most welcome on another of those cloudless desert nights where all earthly heat races off to the icy stars above at the speed of light. I nearly purred along with the idling diesel.

At 0552 I was awakened by perhaps forty explosive beeps from a howitzer located due north. The battle of Samawah had never stopped—Sergeant Kroll says the radio reported another hot firefight in the city through the night. The 1st and 3rd Battalions of the 325th Infantry pushed right up to the Euphrates bridges, not quite halfway into town, apparently killing another dozen gunmen without suffering any casualties of their own. The American artillery rounds we're continuing to hear are being called in by our troopers downtown.

The sun started the day as just a soft, moonlike lozenge on the horizon, but burned hotter and higher with each turret recoil. Now, an hour after cresting land's edge, it reveals its burning truth. No longer masquerading as a passive reflector of someone else's light it announces a hot and airless day ahead. The two-inch-long flying ants which swarm at night disappear, but the flies and biting gnats descend on us in infuriating force.

At one point General Swannack actually tells someone to call the preventive medicine department and have them do something to control the flies in the area. "If PM gets rid of these flies I'll pin a damn medal on them," he roars. The entire swatted-out command staff heartily urges him to make this today's number one battle priority. We may be badly outnumbered, but angry U.S. forces have declared war on their winged nemeses.

After a night of writing, my laptop batteries are flat. So I hike a mile down the road to the FARP where the helicopter battalion is based. I stride the whole way in camel tracks, which are thick as fallen leaves here, and provide solider traction than the uncompacted powdery dust.

First, I get an update in the tiny aviation HQ tent on the last twenty-four hours of aerial work. And then I call once again upon the kindness of Sergeant Bert Foley. The sergeant lived in Seattle for several years, where he developed a loving coffee addiction. He hands out coffee-flavored hard candies mailed over by his wife, and has brought an inverter which converts his Humvee's 24-volt battery to 110-volt power useable by his coffee-maker each morning. Once I discover this, the inverter is also used on more than one afternoon to juice my

Apple. I think of this as rearming my weapon—because when my laptop's dead I'm out of the war.

When the situation reports flow in at the end of the day, it's clear the U.S. military is still very much in a war. This night will feature some of the most concerted bombing of the campaign, with the Air Force planning to drop something like fifteen hundred separate packages, many of them hammering the Medina Division, Saddam's most cohesive tank corps which blocks the southern approach to Baghdad. This is the final preparation for a climactic push to the capital starting tomorrow night. The U.S. 3rd Infantry Division and other units will blast up through the Karbala Pass, which promises a mighty tank battle.

HELLFIRES TO AVOID DAMNATION

APRIL 1—April Fool's Day. I've just spent my second night on the hood. I'm going on a month without running water. I haven't had my current pants or shirt off in more than a week and temperatures are starting to hit one hundred degrees. Even with my new airborne high-taper cut I've got a bad case of helmet hair, and, like others here, I'm getting lots of desert bloody noses. So I guess the joke's on me.

But I'm surrounded by noble spirits. And I managed to shave and give myself a highly satisfying wash this

Know Your Enemy The day after the second Iraq war was kicked off by a cruise missile attack targeting Saddam and his sons, paratroopers from the 82ⁿᵈ Airborne line up at the mess-tent TV in their Kuwait assembly camp to watch an Iraqi broadcast.

Under Missile Attack This infrared photo was taken in the dark inside a Scud bunker during a nighttime missile attack. Soldiers are wearing their gas masks and carrying chemical suits. In the days before the coalition forces burst north into Iraq, nearly a dozen ballistic missiles were launched toward the crowded American camps in northern Kuwait. All threats were knocked down by the Patriot antimissile system.

Leading the Grunts
Colonel Arnold Bray, an imposing 6'6" former college basketball player with a racing mind and tongue, commanded the infantry regiment the 82nd brought to Iraq.

Airborne Instant response to crimes against the nation is the bread and butter of the 82nd Airborne Division. Even their Kiowa attack helicopters can be stuffed into a C-130 transport plane, allowing the division to descend anywhere on the globe within a day's notice. All their war-fighting vehicles and weapons either parachute with them, or airlift in during the first hours of an engagement.

Home in a Bradley Various armored and mechanized units worked beside the 82nd in Bradley Fighting Vehicles like this one. The cramped but fast-moving Bradleys, manned by four soldiers operating a variety of guns, proved to be fearsome American weapons. The wooden crate at this soldier's feet contains dartlike shells tipped with depleted uranium, which can penetrate several inches of armor.

Prepping for Urban Warfare Young troopers from the 325th Infantry get careful training in Kuwait from an experienced Army Ranger on how to handle riots, suicide attacks, and other dangerous civilian disturbances.

War Room Inside the 82ⁿᵈ's new Tactical Operations Center, the digital battle screens offer a mix of top secret maps, intelligence information, and electronic plotting of force positions, as well as public information like news broadcasts. This high-tech control-room-in-a-tent can be broken down and taken anywhere in a day. Using satellite links and portable generators, commanders and officer specialists can control the battlefield and plan new missions from even the most desolate locales.

Battle Masters In the Tactical Operations Center, the commanding general is surrounded by a ring of officers who provide critical information and execute orders from their laptop computers.

Desert Warfare A Humvee from the 82nd races across Iraq's powdery dust as some armor and supply trucks appear in the background. In this vast wasteland there is no place to hide, which is one reason the battalions moved their bases nearly every night.

The Cavalry . . . often guard sites from atop their gun trucks all night long, so when daylight arrives they catch sleep in snatches wherever they can. Note the pistol by the nearest soldier's hands. The brown panel on the side of the Humvee, used to prevent friendly fire accidents, is a special fabric that shows up as a bright glow in American night-vision goggles and thermal weapon sights.

LEFT **Cannon Aid** The business end of a 105mm howitzer. These too can be dropped out of airplanes during the 82nd's parachute assaults, and then used to destroy opposing weapons, fortifications, and troops in support of infantry thrusts.

RIGHT **Why We Fight** On the wall of a captured Iraqi army barracks, commandeered briefly as a headquarters for the 2nd Battalion of the 325th Regiment, some soldier has put up a little reminder of why he is here.

A Soldier's Life Troopers must deal with harsh physical circumstances, and adapt to conditions on the fly. Here, one soldier shaves while another stands guard. Later they will reverse positions.

Feeding the King With one 105mm punch just launched, an artilleryman from the 82nd's 319th Regiment gets ready to shove in another round for firing.

Scouting for Enemies A Kiowa attack helicopter swoops across the barrenness of central Iraq looking for enemies. When the "Wolfpack" pilots spot a target, they loose their rockets, machine guns, or Hellfire missiles. (A Hellfire is mounted low on this chopper, bearing a yellow square.)

Saddam's Jet Bunkers Tallil Air Base, one of Iraq's largest military facilities, was being taken over by new tenants from North Carolina as this image was shot. Pictured here is one of the massive fortified hangars Saddam built to hide his aircraft in. The six-foot concrete walls were no match for U.S. bunker-buster bombs.

World Headquarters of the 82ⁿᵈ Airborne For two nights, this lonely tent in the unsecured central Iraq desert outside of Samawah, guarded by just two dozen men, was the secret battle headquarters of Major General Chuck Swannack and the division staff.

Alpha Troopers Cory Kroll (left), Josh Farley (right), and Chad Stapp (top) man a cavalry gun truck. On top of the Humvee is a TOW missile launcher, a potent weapon with a powerful sight that the gunners especially value for its night optics. On the nights of March 28 and 29, this crew spent tense hours observing an ant farm of human activity in the surrounding desert, while guarding the north flank of the temporary division headquarters pictured on the previous page.

Dawn in Samawah
Well-armed young soldiers from the 2nd Battalion peer tensely down a street in the early moments of a dawn sweep. As one of the Army's elite units, all of the 82nd's infantry have expensive laser aiming sights mounted on the top of their weapons. They rarely miss.

Taking Over Iraqi fedayeen dug fortifications like this foxhole at critical points throughout the city. Until these sites were seized by Americans like this soldier, they were sources of dangerous fire.

Clearing the Streets Second Lieutenant Sean Shields, an Army Ranger, leads a squad sweeping Samawah. Note that he had recorded his blood type on his sleeve, under the patches. Shields is third generation Army Airborne. His father, a retired colonel, participated in the first Gulf War. His grandfather jumped into Normandy and Nijmegen during World War II as a paratrooper in the 82nd Airborne.

Iraqi POWs Iraqi prisoners being held at a desert camp. At the very same time that American POWs were being murdered and abused, these detainees received medical care, food, and shade.

Not Picky Paratroopers from the 3rd Battalion of the 325th lay down to sleep on the dusty platform of the Samawah train station just as the sun comes up, too exhausted after a night of fighting to even take their boots off. The night before they had been positioned to attack the city's main hospital, which guerillas had converted into a command center, but the raid was cancelled by the 82nd's commanders at the last moment, for fear of injuring innocents.

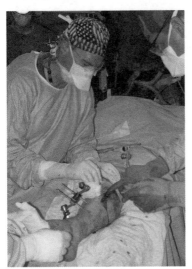

Field Hospital Lieutenant Colonel George Bal and Major Mark Taylor perform surgery on a soldier of the 325th Infantry who was shot in the leg. The day before, they operated on a trooper shot in the face by a ricochet. "He spit out the bullet and some teeth." Field hospital tents must be sealed to keep out desert dirt, so the temperatures soar—I estimate it was at least 130 degrees in this tent during the operation. U.S. Army doctors treated many Iraqi prisoners and civilians as well as American soldiers. Regrettably, Major Taylor was killed in a mortar attack by Iraqi insurgents in March 2004.

Paving the Way Artillery fire, along with Apache attack helicopters and air force bombers and gunships, was used to soften up bunkers, mortar sites, and machine gun nests before the infantry assault over the bridges.

Rock Drill Infantry commanders from the 2nd Battalion of the 325th plan details of their climactic raid in the liberation of Samawah. Using bricks, chunks of cardboard and foam mattress, water bottles, duct tape, and other materials at hand, they have mocked up buildings, roads, trenches, and river to create a 3-D map of the enemy stronghold just north of the Euphrates, where they will attack.

Stoking a Bonfire The paratroopers of Charlie Company, 2nd Battalion of the 325th Regiment, 82nd Airborne Division, are addressed by company commander Captain Adam Carson, shortly before going into combat at Samawah, Iraq, on April 4.

Find Cover Paratroopers run for cover as others peer into a courtyard about to be assaulted during the April 4 raid.

Toast This "technical"—a civilian vehicle with a large gun mounted on the back by irregular forces—was destroyed by the bombardment that immediately preceded the infantry offensive, which began with us dashing over the Euphrates bridge pictured in the background.

Smoking the Fedayeen Fighting rages around some soldiers who have just cleared a building where they found a stash of rocket-propelled grenades. Even with all the U.S. air power and ground technology, the final responsibility for securing the city fell on men working the old-fashioned way: with rifles, pistols, and knives, one room at a time.

House by House Paratroopers from Bravo Company of the 2nd Battalion move down an alley, clearing structures one by one. Iraqi fighters had secreted themselves all through this heavily residential district, and many families discovered inside the buildings had to be relocated to safer areas.

LEFT **Rear Guard** At each intersection, the squad would post a machine gunner and rifleman to provide rear security. The machine gunners also set up along the river when we looped back to it, and fired several times upon irregular troops trying to rush the bridges in commandeered vehicles ranging from taxis to propane trucks.

RIGHT **Discovering the Doctor** One of the houses entered and cleared by the Bravo Company troopers was this one, which occupied a commanding position at one end of a pontoon bridge that needed to be guarded from the rooftop. It turned out the building was occupied by an Iraqi family headed by a doctor, whose services the soldiers soon called upon to try to save an injured boy.

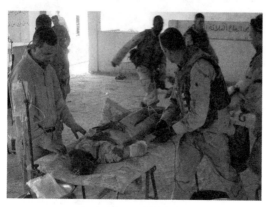

The Cost of Hiding Fighters Among Innocents Here U.S. medics from the 82nd and the Iraqi surgeon (who was too fearful of retribution for cooperating with the Americans to give his name) try to save Bassan's life, after he has been transferred by commandeered bus to an aid station set up in a more secure part of the city.

Out With the Old, In With the New Once American paratroopers swept each building of Iraqi fighters, they would mark it with a C for "Clear." Here they did so right under the eye of the maximum dictator.

Elements of Victory Powered by simple food and water, equipped with superior technology, and guided by good leaders, very young but spirited Americans like southern Californian Josh Farley provided the indefatigable energy, courage, and brainpower that won this war.

morning with two and a half cups of water. So I can't help feeling bubbly.

The uncomplaining stamina and toughness of the cav troopers continues to astound me. As usual, Josh and Chad alternated on two-hour shifts, while the sergeant was on call all night making final judgments. They were glued to their scopes to make sure no one would creep up on us, or lob high explosives onto our heads. By the time they're deployed back home, these guys will have gone literally months without laying in a bed.

This morning I crowd into the tiny command tent with ten other men of the division's headquarters staff, most of us hunching on crates and boxes of water. At 1007 a radio call from Colonel Bray comes in, asking for a surgical strike to take out a building in Samawah. The CIA reports that two high officials of southern Iraq's Baath party are meeting there right now. The structure is also being used as a command post for coordinating attacks by irregulars throughout the city.

But this is a war where the U.S. is taking extraordinary measures to avoid any actions which might hurt innocent people or inflame Iraqi or international opinion. "You know that'll require approval from the four-star level [General Tommy Franks at CentCom headquarters in Qatar]," growls General Swannack. "Have you considered other methods of taking out the building's occupants from your location?" The infantry had, and concluded it would take too long to stage enough foot soldiers to storm the premises. "Let me work on this," the CG concluded tersely.

Instantly, the intelligence officer and judge advocate sprang to check the quality of the intelligence justifying the strike, and to assess the desirability and practicality of such an action. In a whisker, they had the CIA agent on the radio. "It's humint [human intelligence]. We have a source who has proven extremely reliable over the past ten days. Most of the aerial bombing we've called in during that period has been based on his information. We've learned from this source that Muhayfan Halwan, the number-one Baath party official in the Salman region down on the Saudi border has come up to meet with Sultan Al-Sayf, the number-two Baath guy in this region. As of 0915 this morning they were planning future ops in this compound."

Simultaneously, the CG asks for double confirmation and pinpointing of the location of the building from forces on the ground. An intelligence officer in the corner pivots to his laptop and begins to search a database of known Baath party offices to see if there is any match. He checks the known uses of nearby buildings.

"That grid coordinate shows one school a hundred thirty-five meters from the target building, and several others in the area beyond two hundred meters," he relays to the CIA officer.

"Yeah, but since the shooting started school hasn't been meeting in this area. We believe those schools are empty."

On the side, the judge advocate is reminding other officers of this war's rules of engagement. "A building may be fired on if it is a source of active fire or imminent danger. This can even include mosques, whatever, in extreme circumstances. But otherwise the basic ground rule we're operating under is that preplanned destruction of Iraqi buildings—not just sensitive buildings, but *any* building—must be approved at the highest level by Central Command."

Then the CIA agent summarizes his case strongly, "Look, if two heads of the Baath party can be taken out here today, that sends a powerful signal to the enemy. Then your infantry push proceeds to the bridges tonight as planned. And very quickly, resistance looks futile. This could definitely hasten the liberation of Samawah within the next forty-eight hours or so."

EIGHTEEN-POUND HAMMER

After some crosstalk, amidst a cacophony of radioed details, this quickly becomes the consensus position. The CG picks up a handset and explains the request to the staff of General Franks in Qatar. "I'm looking for a precision strike from fixed wing aircraft on grid coordinate NV two-five-six/six-three-five," he concludes.

The JAG suggests that CentCom be informed the building can be lased by a hovering Kiowa Warrior to ensure that the bomb goes exactly where it's wanted, further reducing the chances of any collateral damage. Then the CG jumps in. "Maybe we should just have the Kiowas lob a couple of Hellfires into the building." The communications officer quietly places a call. Across the plain, turbines begin to wind and pilots scramble.

Colonel McDonald, the fire support officer or FSO, draws out the thread: "The smallest Air Force precision bomb has a five-hundred-pound warhead, versus eighteen pounds of high explosive on a Hellfire. If we're looking to minimize risks of destruction overflow, maybe that's enough."

The JAG continues the thinking out loud. "On the other hand, there's a big political and psychological component to this strike, and if we're trying to send a message, a bigger boom is better—so long as we're comfortable we're not gonna get unwanted collateral damage."

Then a new voice, apparently calling from an airplane, rasps across the radio waves. "All-American 6, this is Thunder X-ray. I need to talk to your forward controller about laser illumination versus other means of acquiring the target." This seems to be an AWACS controller, or perhaps even a pilot, getting down to the nitty-gritty. That suggests CentCom approval may be coming, and surprisingly rapidly. In a quick conversation, it appears the munition most easily available is a two thousand-pound satellite-guided bomb.

"I think two thousand pounds might be overkill. If we get approval, let's consider using the Hellfires. Less chance of messing up nearby buildings and houses," states one of the officers.

Just as these final details are being debated there is a beating of Black Hawk rotors and a cloud of dust. Everyone in the tent stands up. Lieutenant General William Wallace, the V Corps commander out of Germany, who currently controls the 82nd Airborne and other divisions in this theater, slides under the tent flap for a previously scheduled update.

First, he's quickly briefed on the possible strike at the Baath officials. As this is happening, Thunder X-ray once again hisses over the radio. It's 1116, a little more than an hour from when the initial request came in, and the strike has been OK'd. But it's been modified based on the preceding discussion. "You are to destroy the building with Hellfires using visual spotting," he crackles from on high.

"OK," begins General Swannack, "based on the size of that building I want you to put at least a couple Hellfires into it to make sure we destroy it." Then he returns to his boss at his elbow. General Wallace is extremely softspoken, almost mute. He seems gravely tired. The discussion between the generals turns to current operations to free Samawah.

An anecdote that came in from Colonel Bray this morning is passed along. A young boy presented himself to soldiers from the 325th with a note from his father in broken English offering to share information on the location and operations of the guerrillas. Details would have to await the arrival of an interpreter, but the colonel explained that this was just one of a surge of incidents suggesting the city's populace was coming to trust American intentions and would be cooperating more and more.

Some unconfirmed intelligence is laid out for the visiting general: There are sketchy reports that suicide teams are arriving from Syria and Lebanon; the suicide attacks seen so far may be the work of people other than Iraqis. There are hints that up to half of all the fighters previously in the city may have given up or fled the area. A major explains that this is based on signals intelligence—information intercepted in a newly launched program to monitor local cell phones.

Then the 82nd's CG spins toward his FSO, who is on the line with the helicopter battalion. "All right, what's the status of the Hellfire shoot?"

"Sir, the KWs [Kiowa Warriors] are inbound now."

"How many Hellfires are they hauling?"

"Four missiles, sir. They're going to fire them all and we'll see what happens." (That'll make it a big event for the pilots I've been hanging with. Each Hellfire costs about as much as a Mercedes.)

"Right. Immediately after the shoot I want a DA [damage assessment] so we can see the results."

"Will do, sir."

Now we can hear the pilots on the radio. "Red Wolf to All-American: approaching site."

"Roger, let me know when you have a shot."

The room falls silent, awaiting a denouement. The two generals, who clearly have no more than a formal relationship, sit uneasily shoulder-to-shoulder, sending parallel stares silently down at the map that's taped to the table in front of them. We all listen to the rasping communication between the pilots.

"Still trying to get a shot?" presses the CG.

"Just seconds, sir. Just seconds."

But in truth it's more like minutes, and then more minutes. "Let's hope Baath leaders like to linger over their tea," someone cracks.

Now the Black Hawks are spooling up. General Wallace is going to have to depart for his next hop. Both commanders step out of the tent, gusting a wave of accumulated tension out between the flaps with them.

THE GENTLEST WAR

After seeing off his superior officer, General Swannack slips back in. At 1152 the radio finally offers a live report from the pilots: "Two missiles fired." Then a minute later. "Third missile in." An awkward hesitation, then more reporting from the air, with the pilot speaking in an excited tone: "A pickup truck just raced away from the side entrance. Three individuals inside. There's another empty truck on the other side. Should I engage it?"

Momentary whirring of mental wheels, then two or three officers blurt out the same thing. "No! Save that last missile. Go find and engage the truck with the men in it. Leave the empty one alone."

The FSO relays that instruction, but almost right away a reply comes back. "Negative. Truck proceeded only one block north, and then turned into side streets."

"In other words, they lost him," summarizes someone, with disappointment in his voice.

"See if you can reacquire that vehicle," says the CG with surprising calm. But a few minutes later it's clear the truck and its occupants are long gone. The damage assessment: clean holes in the side of the building, no secondary explosions. No building collapse. No knowledge of who escaped, who was stopped inside.

"Looks like we needed a bigger punch," says General Swannack quietly.

And so ended another judicious—probably too judicious—application of force by the U.S. military. What I witnessed were extraordinary efforts to avoid cracking any innocent eggs. In the end, smaller rather than larger weapons were selected. And as a result, the bad guys may have gotten away. (Or maybe not. It does appear the strike made someone angry—fedayeen mortars flung several rounds in our direction within minutes of the loosing of the Hellfires.)

Such are the tough choices and uncertainties of a war

being conducted with unusual restraint, and even gentleness, by commanders aiming to be accepted as saviors rather than conquerors. It is a pattern I've seen recur over and over again in this fight. The real story of the Iraq War thus far, I suggest, has been the leverage the U.S military has foregone, not the leverage it has applied. Our leaders have been shooting for the hearts and minds of everyday Iraqis as much as for the gangsters of the Baath party, and military officers have willingly fought with their hands tied in the interest of sparing civilians. Anyone who tells the world otherwise is just plain wrong.

THE KING SPEAKS

In late afternoon, while I was on my satellite phone dictating a story for publication back home, I heard a loud explosion quite nearby, and then saw a plume rising hundreds of feet into the air behind the headquarters tent, which obscured my view of the impact site. Soldiers were throwing on body armor; others raced up with their rifles to take positions along the four-foot-high earth berm of an old agricultural canal bounding the immediate rear of our camp here. I hung up and stepped into the command center.

Almost immediately a familiar voice popped onto the radio. It was Sergeant Kroll, reporting that immediately after the incoming round landed on the plain in front of his Humvee, Farley spotted several trucks in his TOW sight fleeing a location between us and Samawah. I grinned to myself. My boys out there were watching our back.

The software on the radars set up by the division's 319th Artillery Regiment identified the projectile (based on warhead speed, size, and parabola) as likely coming from a D-30 howitzer, a formidable weapon that the Iraqi forces in Samawah were not at that point known to possess. The D-30 has a range of over fifteen kilometers. We were sitting on an open plain about twelve kilometers from the city.

At this point the FSO got up and put on his helmet. The artillery radars are not foolproof, and sometimes give false readings. Others in the tent began to josh that he seemed a little too nervous. "Hey, you can do what you want," he ribbed right back, "but I know the King [his affectionate term for the power of heavy artillery]. I respect the King. I've seen what the King can do. And I'm putting on my damn Kevlar."

Later, inspection of the crater and other factors suggested the round was more likely a mortar. Probably launched by those characters whose south sides Josh Farley saw while they were fleeing north. Or perhaps by some of the other creepy crawlies the Alpha Troopers and I had been watching through the thermal sight the last two nights. The CG asked that a combat patrol check out the locale of the fleeing trucks for weapons caches or other evidence that it might be a site in need of further watching.

HOT NIGHTS FOR THE 325th

SAMAWAH, IRAQ, APRIL 2—I'm now with the infantrymen of the 325th Regiment of the 82nd. The 2nd Battalion has taken up residence in what used to be a barracks of the Iraqi Army. The compound is a ruin, but it's surrounded by a wall, the buildings have roofs, and after a week out in the dust it seems comparatively luxurious. Unfortunately these men have no mission planned for the night, so I hop a ride on a truck full of water bottles and MREs that is headed, with armed escort, over to the 3rd Battalion headquarters a few kilometers away, in the city's abandoned train station. On the way we pass several M-1 tanks guarding bridges and entry points.

Third Battalion has been doing some of the heaviest fighting in the city up to now. "Last night, when we assaulted the major bridges crossing to the north side of the Euphrates River we were involved in a really heavy firefight," a Lieutenant Bryant tells me. "Hotter than Operation Anaconda in Afghanistan, hotter than anything any U.S. forces have encountered in a lot of years. The Special Republican Guard and the paramilitaries had dug in a large number of machine guns, mortars, RPGs, weapons of all sorts, just over the bridges. Bullets were flying everywhere. We had rounds landing forty feet from the colonel's Humvee. They really opened up on us for several hours. But we punched back and killed a large number of them, and took many prisoners."

At one point, an ambulance roared up to a Samawah checkpoint, its lights popping and siren screaming. An infantryman fired a warning shot to bring it to a halt (just as the troops have been instructed to do), but as the ambulance screeched to a stop, four irregulars jumped out with guns blazing. Because the guard's alertness prevented the vehicle from getting closer, no soldier was killed; the gunmen were. Ambulances are also being used as couriers—for orders, arms, and fighters—so the troopers have learned to watch them suspiciously.

At about the same time, we learned that some of the holiest religious sites in Iraq, in Najaf and Karbala, are being used as firing points by Saddam's gunmen. With each new outrage, the fedayeen increase the chances of drawing innocent people into the war.

Another low blow was struck that same day at a building on the east side of Samawah. It had been identified as a source of enemy fire, so one of the forward air controllers out with the troops called in an airstrike. The bomber was actually overhead and about to let fly when the Iraqi fighters in the building literally ran into the street and grabbed a number of terrified women and children, dragging them into the building with them. The air drop was instantly called off, and a decision was made by U.S. commanders to leave the building alone for the moment.

Also on April 2, a large number of armed guerrillas congregated in a stadium and adjoining abandoned school. Shots were exchanged. Then the 319th Artillery was called in, and howitzer rounds flew fast and furious.

Earlier, an armored cavalry Humvee—identical to the one I've been riding in and sleeping on for the past three days, and undoubtedly manned by the same kind of sturdy and jovial men I've encountered throughout the cavalry—was in Samawah. While rolling along a road it was blasted from behind by a rocket-propelled grenade. One U.S. soldier from a cavalry unit supporting the 82nd was killed, and two crew members were wounded.

A RAID DEFERRED

SAMAWAH TRAIN STATION—The good news is that this cavalryman was the only American soldier killed in Samawah this week. A dozen or so Americans have been wounded and treated at one of the impressive field hospital tents I've visited, where hardy Army doctors practice an amazingly high quality of medicine without benefit of running water, disinfected operating rooms, refrigeration, or other niceties. The most delicate cases are of course forwarded quickly to more sophisticated hospitals aboard Navy ships or at bases in Europe.

Meanwhile, an average of fifteen to twenty enemy guerrillas are being killed daily. More are being taken prisoner. I observed perhaps fifty Iraqi POWs being held temporarily behind wire when I was at the brigade headquarters. Interviewers are reportedly getting some good information from them about activities of the irregulars in the city, many or even most of whom are apparently fanatics who have arrived from outside points.

Not yet fully convinced they are finally free of Saddam, local residents remain tentative about cooperating openly with the American soldiers. But they are starting to believe. Last night, several Iraqis loitering along a rail bed grinned and waved at us as our column of five military vehicles passed.

The mission I came to the 3rd Battalion to observe tonight was the storming of a four hundred-bed hospital that the fedayeen have been using as a battle headquarters. This repeats the same dastardly pattern followed in Nasiriyah, where the Marines eventually had to seize a hospital that had become a guerrilla command center. They uncovered not only military plans and stores, but also a large stash of gas masks and atropine injectors, intended for use by local military and political bosses in the event their field commanders unleashed a chemical attack.

Our 3rd Battalion now had the Samawah hospital cordoned off. Snipers were picking off soldiers who could be seen at the windows holding weapons. A forced entry was the next step.

But shortly after dark, the mission was canceled—out of fear of injuring bystanders. Not knowing whether patients were inside, or how many, the assault was put on hold. The American commanders would simply put up with attacks organized out of the hospital rather than risk hurting civilians. "Like the Bible says, 'we know not the hour, we know not the day'—but we do know we are going to prevail. So we're willing to be patient to avoid hurting innocent people," Colonel Bray had explained some days earlier when describing how he would choose his fights.

So instead of joining the nighttime raid, I lay down in an empty porter's room within the ruined Samawah train station. A flea-bitten old couch in one corner had long since been robbed of its seat cushions, but the back padding was still there. I kicked the frame apart and lay down on my first soft surface in weeks.

Strangely, I slept much worse than on the truck hood. Partly, it was the sounds of combat roaring around me. Shortly after I lay down, the whining tremors of a long column of tanks and armored personnel carriers drew near, eventually passing just on the other side of the tracks from the train platform where I lay. Then at 2155 the mortars outside the front door of the station began to fire heavily on some target, joined by a second artillery battery somewhere close at hand. After perhaps fifteen minutes the barrage stopped, bringing a stupefying silence.

At some point in the black night there was a tremendous explosion very near by, which I less heard than felt in my throat and groin. I lay wondering: An ammunition cache going up? An incoming shell? Who knows? No one stirred in other parts of the station, so I rolled over; just one more bit of wartime din.

Then a few hours before dawn, the troopers who had been pre-positioned for the canceled raid poured into our station in a soft glow of green chem lights and the clanking of a hundred rifles and rucksacks. Within minutes, most had laid down on the concrete train siding, curled against their packs and ponchos and each other, boots still on, and fallen sound asleep. Amid the '40s-era railcars parked beside them, and under the vintage platform clock frozen in time above them, they resembled generations of grunts from the conductor-and-locomotive era.

Giving up on sleep myself, I splashed some water on my face and opened a Murray (as soldiers sometimes call MREs). One trooper had rescued from a garbage heap an eight-inch pup of the mangy curs that wander much of Iraq. As I sat on a broken marble step it repeatedly tried to nose into my breakfast. This dog deserved a cuff. Somehow, though, I couldn't bring myself to slap it.

6

FINAL ASSAULT

BAGHDAD DRESS REHEARSAL

BACK AT THE SAMAWAH IRAQI ARMY BARRACKS, APRIL 3—Some of what the men of the 325th Regiment have been doing this week is basic infantry blocking and tackling, but much of it is the more delicate and tricky work of urban warfare—clearing intersections and buildings, taking and holding bridges, draining sniper's nests, smashing mortar and machine gun sites hidden in residential neighborhoods. To date, this has been done with extraordinary success, measured by the enemy-to-friendly kill rate.

In the first war with Iraq, Kuwait was liberated and

most of the Iraqi military destroyed at a cost of 293 Americans killed, and 467 wounded. Those are extraordinarily light losses for the work accomplished. But of course that was basically a desert tank war that was halted short of cities like Samawah and Baghdad. Guerrilla street fighting can be a great equalizer, and there is a rule of thumb that any force battling its way into a city can expect casualties of up to a third.

When down the road in Nasiriyah the Marines carried out operations similar to those now taking place in Samawah, they got stung, taking many more casualties than have so far accumulated here. Was the resistance fiercer? Are the tactics employed in Samawah better? Is the 82nd doing something especially well?

The 82nd has always claimed a special expertise in urban warfare. "You've got to understand, every officer in this division closely studies the classic urban battles, from the Israeli case histories right back to Stalingrad," states Lieutenant Barbato when I ask about this. "We train all the time for clearing airport terminals and other public spaces. So we're ready for this."

It occurs to me that the 82nd's sweep of Samawah may very well be the dress rehearsal for a final performance of the same script, on a larger scale, in Baghdad. If Iraq's capital can be pacified with the same minimal losses of life that have so far occurred here, it will be an enormous achievement. Those urban warfare textbooks will have to be revised, and the men of the 82nd will be writing history as well as reading it.

Time will tell.

While reflecting on this, I got wind that the climactic raid of the 82nd Airborne's liberation of Samawah will take place starting around midnight tonight, culminating in an infantry assault across the bridges spanning the Euphrates. The dense north side of the river—the stronghold of the guerrillas who had poured withering fire onto the 325th during the first push to take the bridges two days earlier—will now be frontally attacked and occupied.

This time the 3rd Battalion, which has borne much of the infantry work to date, is going to rest and regroup. The assault will be conducted by the 1st and 2nd Battalions, which is why I've jumped a supply convoy back to the headquarters of the 2nd.

The men will be preceded over the bridges by Bradleys and other armored vehicles from the 41st Infantry Regiment, assigned to support the 82nd here. The 82nd's artillery, plus AC-130 gunships, will also bombard the riverfront bunkers and buildings where many of the machine guns, mortars, and RPG firing positions are dug in. And Apache and Kiowa helicopters will be in the air with us, armed with missiles, rockets, and machine guns.

That is all any foot soldier could ever hope for. But the final responsibility for sweeping the streets and cleaning out the buildings—one room at a time—is going to fall on men working the old-fashioned way: with rifles, pistols, and knives.

TOY SOLDIERS

Just before any grassroots infantry assault takes place, U.S. Army units always run what is called a "rock drill." This is a kind of low-tech war game, where enemy and friendly forces are laid out on the floor of a tent or building, along with symbols for landmarks, roads, and geographical features. Then company and platoon commanders walk through the battle plan, deciding the nitty-gritty of who will attack which objective, from what direction, with what lines of fire, and so on.

The "rock drill" name comes from the fact that these are traditionally staged using stones, sticks, sand—whatever the fighters can lay their hands on at the battlefield. In our case, the 3-D scenario was set up in one room of the commandeered Iraqi Army barracks where we were squatting, using bricks, cardboard cut from boxes, fabric curtain strips to represent roads, and chunks of foam sliced off mattresses. Parachute cord tied to water bottles delineated the map grid lines that would show up on each platoon's GPS locator. Critical buildings that needed to be seized were code-named for U.S. presidents. Vital roads and alleys were given titles of different automobiles. Duct tape indicated the location of trenches through which the fedayeen would flow to the battle zone. In addition, sheaves of blown-up aerial maps of the neighborhood were distributed to squad leaders— quite a short-order feat in these squalid surroundings, accomplished with portable generators and wide-format printers hooked to laptop computers holding various defense intelligence topo maps on their hard drives.

Time was tight. The stakes were high. At 1700, twenty mostly young commanders and squad leaders clustered around the floor map in a sweaty circle. The tone was hard, the language brutal, the pace racing.

It had been learned that Karim Hamdany, a member of Saddam Hussein's inner circle and a four-star uniformed general in the Republican Guard, had come down from Baghdad to organize the local resistance. Street intersections had been built up with fighting positions. Machine gun nests were dug in and sandbagged in many locations. RPGs and ammunition were stashed in scores of buildings across the northern neighborhoods.

Guerrillas would be secreted among innocent townspeople, whom they would use for cover. "This town is about to turn," explained the operations officer. "Lots of people are excited. We've got friendly locals waving at and approaching our patrols now. But this actually causes problems, because the irregulars mix in with them to get close, then drop a grenade or an RPG onto a Humvee. This is a dangerous phase. We've got PsyOp teams broadcasting on the streets now, telling people that the coalition forces are conducting risky operations and that they need to stay in their homes to be safe. We'll keep putting out that message, and for now anyone who approaches you has to be considered a potential enemy. Be on guard at all times."

Hot spots, choke points, and problem buildings are

identified. Decisions are made on which squads should attack each. Snipers are assigned positions on high buildings. There is heavy emphasis on the rules of engagement, on fields of fire and physical operational limits, all of which are carefully calibrated to avoid fratricide or collateral civilian damage.

The infantry will mount open stake trucks starting around 2230 tonight. The vehicles will drive under blackout conditions to a location a few kilometers from the attack zone. Troopers will then dismount and silently walk the remaining distance using their night-vision goggles. Just before dawn there will be a three hundred meter sprint across a metal bridge, with the assault to begin immediately upon reaching the north bank of the Euphrates River.

Second Battalion's Charlie Company will spearhead the fight. Alpha and Bravo Company will work on the right and left flanks. And the Delta Company troopers in Humvees with Mark 19s and other heavy roof-mounted guns will provide cover and engage any heavy enemy weapons or "technicals" that show up. ("Technical" is the military term for a civilian vehicle that has been modified into a mobile gun truck.) I'm going in with Charlie Company.

BUILDING A BONFIRE

After the rock drill, commanders go back to their companies and platoons and brief them on their assignments. The battle plan rapidly trickles down to each part of the fighting machine. Small squads working with flashlights and headlamps hash out final details and rehearse movements.

Then a yellow glow begins to build in a barracks courtyard. This is unusual. We have operated, necessarily, under strict light discipline during our whole time in Iraq, with either no night illumination allowed, or just red or green pinlights. The glow is fast becoming an orange-red roar, toward which we all instinctively begin to shift. As a captain pushes past me I hear him murmur, "Holy shit, I ask five privates to build me a campfire and this is what I get!"

A giant pyre now rages, fueled by several foam mattresses some enthusiastic young pyromaniacs have tossed into the flames. In a land of wood, this bonfire would be a terror. But Iraq is not a land of wood; it is a land of dust and sand and broken concrete.

Charlie Company is ordered to fall in. Painted red by firelight and ferocity, one hundred twenty men form in neat ranks. "At ease men. Gather around me," barks Captain Adam Carson. Carson has been company commander for one year and three months. He saw his first combat three days earlier. But he is prepared.

"You," he pauses for emphasis, "are all part of history.

After that nasty firefight at the bridges two days ago, you have already seen more combat than any unit of the 82nd Airborne since the 1960s. Now we're going to finish that job.

"I need guys who can hit targets. I need guys who will do anything to protect their buddies. I need guys who are ready to kill.

"Unlike last time, we're going in tonight with some armor. And Apaches. And with Delta Company. I'm gonna be damn glad to have the Delta boys with us. We're gonna need them. But gun trucks stand out. They can get cornered on tight city streets. They're a juicy target for an RPG.

"If one of those trucks gets hit, I want you to treat it like a damn downed helicopter. I want you to run to that vehicle and get everybody out. We're not leaving anybody behind, understand?

"And I want you to remember something. You are Americans. Americans don't shoot women and children. They don't kill soldiers who have surrendered. That's what the assholes we're up against do. That's what we're fighting. We're gonna do things differently.

"But if your life is in danger, you shoot. And you shoot to kill."

A quiet burst of "hoo-ah"—the airborne cry of enthusiasm and seriousness—rises from the circle of men.

The commander ends by reading Psalm 144, with its tribute to those who battle against unrighteousness. "How's everyone feeling?"

Instantly, a roaring "HOO-AH" surges from one hundred twenty throats.

CRACK SHOT

After being dismissed, the soldiers wolf down some quick food and as much water as they can drink, then find a corner where they can stretch out in the dust for a little sleep. Most troopers remain amazingly loose. I ask one soldier if I can perch on a comfortable ledge next to him. "Roger," he answers. "It's a free country. Or at least it's fixing to be."

I eventually settle my backpack next to Sergeant Patrick Duhon, a proud Cajun from Abbeville, Louisiana, and Sergeant Chad Meggison, a radio operator from Waverly, Illinois. We're joined by Air Force Sergeant Donnavon Huss, one of about forty forward air controllers assigned to accompany the various field commanders of the 82nd Airborne to call in airstrikes from the F-15s, F-14 Tomcats, and myriad other aircraft circling invisibly overhead most of the day and night.

"Old Hollywood was in his element tonight, huh?" suggests Duhon, using Captain Carson's universal nickname. "Yeah, he did all right," the others agree quietly. This is a flinty trio, not easily impressed. They are veteran fighters with experience in Afghanistan, Bosnia, and many points in between.

Huss shows me the black laser illuminator he uses to

guide bombs dropped from miles above the earth onto targets as precisely as a dentist puts in a filling. The size and shape of a common flashlight, and powered by just four AA batteries, the laser can inscribe a brilliant spot on a building a mile away. The light is of a frequency invisible to humans not wearing NODs, but the pointer will blind anyone it hits in the eyes, so we scan the horizon carefully with his goggles before he lets me play at marking a distant water tower with the device.

The banter among the sergeants turns to an amazing shot made a day or two earlier by a sniper with the 2nd Battalion, Specialist Robert Stewart. The group had been tasked to seize the Samawah water treatment plant. While perched on a high tower on a nearly moonless night, Stewart scoped, all the way across the city, the silhouette of a man with an RPG strapped to his back. The man was moving on the roof of a building, and visible only in flickering outline. Using a .50 caliber rifle in the seated position, Stewart lined up his shot. Duhon, Meggison, and Huss watched him squeeze the trigger.

Even with the high muzzle velocity of the .50 caliber, it took more than two full seconds after the gun fired before the bullet arrived at its target. Suddenly, the guerrilla slumped and rolled off his building. Stunned, the sergeants checked the grid locations. A 1,440-meter rifle shot—a colossal achievement that got Stewart written up the next day for a medal nomination. (I learned later that he will receive the Bronze Star.)

"Man, you might as well call that a one-mile plug," suggested one of the men.

"Until that moment, the most amazing shot I ever saw was one taken by my daddy. We live in a rural area, all surrounded by fields, and my dad looked out a bathroom window and saw a coyote trotting up a hillside. He let out a holler and ran for his Browning. I followed him out into the yard. Almost immediately the coyote got wind of us and started to hauling. That coyote was at a dead run when dad let fly. Lord, that dog flipped in the air three times before he landed. We walked it off: five hundred paces. My dad can shoot."

PHANTASM

EVENING, APRIL 3—Soon, men have settled themselves quietly on the ground in a handful of pods. Only the radio operators and a few others are still fine-tuning their equipment. For most, weapons have long since been cleaned and loaded, magazines stacked, canteens filled. Several soldiers are privately writing things by pinlight. I think I know what. Heavy breaths and scattered snoring mark the lucky men.

The early night soon grows phantasmagoric. In the dark overhead, a sonic catalogue of various aircraft noises rapidly builds. A few miles off, bombs begin to burst, and missiles whir. The light show reaches a peak when the 105mm cannon of an AC-130—a kind of tank, Bradley, and gun truck all in one flying package—begins to rip.

In a circle all around our camp, the infernal hounds of Iraq begin their horrible yipping, choking, yowling barks. Some squeal as if caught in the jaws of some other dog; perhaps they are. The wheezing and gas-passing of the men increases. Some of the dreamers are ejaculating names and bizarre fragments of phrases in their disturbed somnolence.

The burning foam mattresses, which seemed such a bold stroke an hour ago, are now just a source of reeking stink. "That smell is gonna kill me," someone mutters. Now the artillery, very nearby, follows the Air Force into explosive action. The dog howling crescendos. I find myself fantasizing that Sergeant Huss has called in an airstrike to silence their aggressive mawing. A B-52 carpet-bombing to restore the audial peace.

Then everything outside the city goes quiet. In the fresh silence I begin to detect a new sound: the clanking creak of tank treads. The armored vehicles of the 41st are now moving into the lair of the Samawah guerrillas. These are gentler, more distant sounds. But they do not relent.

The hours crawl. Finally, hands are shaking men awake.

MURPHY VERSUS FUDGE

As we shed our grogginess, the radios hiss a new installment in the ancient tale of Army bureaucracy. Someone
has screwed up. A group of the trucks needed to transport five hundred soldiers were sent to a wrong grid. No
one knows where they are now.

Some other trucks were sent out with no sides on
them. Heavily laden paratroopers can't perch on the flat
bed of a high-mobility truck rocking and rolling over off-
road obstacles. The abidingly cynical belief that many
soldiers have in the power of Murphy's Law (If something can go wrong, it will) now kicked into high gear.

"What a joke. This is like freakin' leg land," spluttered
the company commander. "Here we are the 82nd Airborne, the most deployable unit in the U.S. military, an
elite outfit that prides itself on being able to throw
thousands of guys and tons of vehicles out of airplanes
anywhere in the world within hours, and we can't get
forty frigging trucks organized on a full day's notice! The
friggin' GACs [truck convoys] are *always* the weak link.
I told you it'd turn into a goat f__k." He stops pacing and
turns to me. "And you can quote me on that."

Fortunately, the night is rescued by another ancient
Army tradition—the fudge factor. The original plan had
everyone piling into trucks way too early anyway, so
there turns out to be plenty of time to track down the
wayward vehicles, refit those without sides, and com-
mandeer some from elsewhere.

As the only person in the horde without NODs, I am desperately trying to hang with the Charlie Company radio operators during the mob movement to the trucks in pitch blackness. I fail. I run into a trooper who asks where I'm from, and when I tell him upstate New York he says he's a Cornell graduate. What the hell, I'll join his group; and so I end up with the Charlie mortar team. We all clamber seven feet up some ladders and flop ourselves, laden with body armor, water, weapons and ammo (for the soldiers) and photo equipment (for me), over tailgates.

"The last part of the trip, we're going to be off the hardball [paved road], and cuttin' cross-country over a dicey stretch," warns the convoy master on the radio. He urges the drivers, who will be navigating with night-vision goggles, which is tricky, to proceed slowly to avoid rollovers. He warns troopers to hang on tight, and not to be surprised if we take fire entering the city limits. The soldiers remain wondrously cool. Quite bold. And highly amusing.

COMEDY NIGHT

Even with the trucking foibles, it develops that in order to make the timing work for the dawn attack, we have to sit in our switched-off vehicles about an hour before departing. This turns out to be, without question, the most hilarious hour of my life. Sitting in pitch darkness, well into the hallucinatory hours of the night, crammed together like sardines, and in a highly reflective mood, the sardonic potential was there right from the get-go.

Soon, splashing sounds could be heard. "Hey buddy, your truck is leaking," hollered someone. Before long, bladders were venting all around us, in eight-foot streams over the side rails.

"I kinda want to smoke a cigarette," complains one soldier wryly, as he sits next to Lieutenant Ney. "And then again, statistics show that eighty percent of night-time sniper hits are to the faces of smokers, and I sure don't want to get shot in the face by an Iraqi. Then again, we know Iraqi snipers have very bad aim. But then again, I don't want to get Lieutenant Ney shot in the face."

There is some extended riffing about MREs. "My favorite variety is Restroom Rice and Beans," drawled one soldier, kicking off several minutes of foul wordplay on the names of the dishes printed on each container.

"One of the funniest things this whole damn deployment was watching those POWs eat MREs."

"Yeah, I had to 'bout jump to keep one guy from eating the anti-spoilage Dry Pak inside a Pop-Tarts wrapper."

"And I thought you was trying to kill that one prisoner, in direct violation of the Geneva Convention, when you gave him that fudge brownie without any water to drink."

"Yeah, those things are tough as woodpecker lips."

———

"Man, my wife's birthday is coming up. When I was deployed in Egypt I missed it, and I'll tell you what, she has never let me forget that to this day. So I don't care if I have to personally pillage one of Saddam's palaces, I am not going to leave this godforsaken country until I have begged, bought, or stolen something very flashy for my girl."

"Yeah, well I got the opposite problem. My wife is always mailing me all this crap I can't use and can't carry, teddy bears and dumb-ass stuff like that. When I was in Bosnia, I just gave it all away to Albanians."

(Interjected from across the truck: "I bet a nickel some of them ate the stuffed animals.")

"Anyway, when I come home my wife wants to know, all shocked, where all this heartwarming memorabilia has got to, and why I weren't huggin' it close to my chest all the way across the Atlantic Ocean. So now I'm afraid to dump anything, or I'll catch it. I'm goin' have to tell her: If I can't eat it, or wash with it, or use it, don't send it. If it's fuzzy, *definitely* don't send it."

"I had a little fun with my wife just before we left our e-mail back in Kuwait. I sent her a digital photo of some sorry donkey shack. Told her I was in Iraq, and real impressed with the country, and that prices on real estate were awful reasonable right now, given the war and all. Said I'd signed papers for this little country place—needs a bit of work—using half our savings. True, it's a twenty-five-hundred-mile commute to work, but I'll be retiring from the military someday, and then she and I can fix the place up."

"Buddy, I hope you've got a truly loving wife."

"You know what's startin' up about now back home? High school baseball. Boy, I miss that."

"I tried to get a baseball team going at Fort Bragg, but—get this—they told me it was too dangerous. I'm thinking: Wait a minute. Here we are in the Army. Jumping out of airplanes. Shooting at each other. And baseball is too dangerous?"

"Yup, I miss baseball, too. The outfield boundary at my little old high school was danged barbed wire. And cows on the other side. If a game came up and your arm was too sore to pitch, you'd go out that night and drop the wire, and next mornin' there'd be cowpies all over the infield. Game'd get rescheduled, and you could be rested."

"How big was your high school?"

"Graduating class of thirty-six."

"Yeah, my graduating class was twenty-eight. And several of them were charity cases."

"Mine was forty-two. I guess that makes me a big-city boy in this group."

"Well, I'm sure my high school baseball team is going to stink this year, because there were only fourteen seniors in the school."

"That's all right. Hey, that's big. My senior class was eight. I French-kissed seventy-five percent of the senior-class girls before I graduated, and sixty-six percent of the girls in the junior class."

"Why, Sergeant, I didn't realize you were home schooled."

"Don't you mess with me, Private. I'm a dangerous man, and currently armed to the teeth."

GRUFF INTIMACY

At about this time, Sergeant Doak began singing softly over the radio. "Sergeant Doak's Country Convoy Song," with custom lyrics set to the tune of "Ring of Fire."

> *My truck's on fire . . .*
> *Oooh, my, my,*
> *Yes, my truck's on fire . . .*
> *And my legs are both asleep . . .*

Someone rips the sergeant for his lame rhyming. Someone else criticizes his grammar. "You're absolutely right, son," comes an answer, "we simply cannot tolerate a person using incorrect English while heading off to blow things up in combat."

This is followed by some very hairy, ribald, and side-splitting stories about parachute jumps gone wrong. And on and on. I've never witnessed a moment in time more spontaneously, morbidly, and fiercely funny. I couldn't write fast enough in the dark to capture more than just a fragment of the wry folksiness and hilarious banter.

Despite—or perhaps because of—the certainty of gunfire before morning, everyone was "loose as a scrotum in an August overall," as one trooper put it. These men really opened up (in the ways that gruff males do). There was enormous affection and love in the air: love of family, love of home communities and regions of the country, love of the outdoors, love of freedom, love of each other.

Cigarettes were quietly passed back and forth between seatmates. Water bottles were shared. Soldiers automatically, wordlessly, hand a portion of whatever they have to others around them. Preparing for and facing battle, I believe, deepens portions of the soldier's soul, encouraging forms of generosity, empathy, mutual respect, and friendship as no other occupation can.

Outsiders have no idea how much intimacy and hearty comradeship exists between fighting men. Direct reliance on each other for their very survival encourages blunt openness and genuine familial spirit. If there is a corner of modern life where boundaries between men (like race and economics) melt away more completely than in the military, I have never seen it.

GOING IN

CENTER CITY SAMAWAH, APRIL 4—At 0215 we finally roll out of camp. Instantly, the mood turns sober, and all business. Four troopers on each side of the truck pull security—facing outward, their rifles pointed over the siderails, staring into the gloam with their night goggles to search for threats. A SAW (squad automatic weapon) gunner is placed at the tailgate.

When his sergeant notices the machine gunner starting to drowse he jumps on him: "Morton, you asleep?"

A slow and unconvincing "No" comes back.

"Because if I look down at you and find you're asleep," the sergeant whispers fiercely, "I'm gonna shove my foot so far up your ass you're gonna have to swallow to get it back down your throat. We're in a hot zone. Is that clear?"

"Yes, Sarge!"

Murphy is still lurking. The convoy route is a bushwhack chosen to snake us toward the town center while mostly avoiding populated areas, and the scout team has marked the turns only with faint chemical lights laying on the ground. Driving in the total blackout, several trucks pass one turnoff before realizing they're lost. Fortunately they're able to circle around and rejoin the main column. A little farther down the road, however, one of the top-heavy five-ton trucks cuts a corner too tightly and rolls down an incline. Miraculously, nobody's killed. We grind on, abandoning the vehicle.

At 0345 we de-truck. The pre-assault fire from the air and the howitzers is culminating. We see fiery red darts in the sky above us that mean there is an Apache helicopter up there loosing rockets. Then, suddenly, all falls silent.

At 0435 we start to creep into the heart of Samawah, guns ready, NODs on. Goggleless, I stick like a shadow to one bulky sergeant in the mortar group to avoid getting separated or falling into a hole. Thirty minutes later we reach our bridge. There is just enough dawning light now to see without goggles. We start to run.

The air suppression has worked, the company takes no fire on the bridge. We pour over the embankment on the other side and the lead squads fan out, kicking in the first doors and windows, climbing onto roofs.

Immediately, the shooting and explosions start. The mortar man next to me drops the heavy base of his tube. I stoop and pick it up and we run forward together, past a pickup with a large gun mounted on its bed, already charred black by some American soldier or pilot, until the sergeant screams "Set up there!" Readings are immediately taken and fed into the handheld firing computer, and trajectory angles are shouted to the teams at the two tubes. In about three minutes, they are ready for firing.

There is shouting and gunfire directly in front of us.

"Enemy!"

"West building!"

"Taking fire!"

"Hit him! That bastard needs to die!"

A boom of C4 plastic explosive, and another door is down. Very quickly, several rooms and then whole buildings right at the base of the bridge have been cleared. They are spray painted with a large orange C to tell soldiers following that they contain no enemy.

Bent over double, the vanguard elements race to the next building, and then the next. New companies move in behind us. The fan spreads, fluttering only where soldiers pause to dodge bullet sprays and RPG explosions.

BLOCK BY BLOCK

I run, and duck, and take notes, and shoot photographs as light allows. Troopers speak to me several times during the morning. "You're crazy man!" "What'cha doing this for?" "Who made you come here, dude?"

A hole is blown in the wall of one large building which looks like a school. It takes perhaps a half hour to clear the structure of fighters. One of the Delta gun trucks blazes away with its Mark 19 grenade launcher to finish the job.

Further down the street, we enter what looks like it might have been a mosque. The defenders have fled.

Several ominous-looking RPGs they left behind are lying on the ground floor.

As the lead platoons split up and head in separate directions at successive intersections, the soldiers diffuse to the point where squads of just a half-dozen or dozen find themselves working alone over several blocks. I have ended up with a group of about ten men from Bravo Company who cut behind the mosque into a residential district near the river.

The alleys are narrow, and dark windows and doors threaten from every direction. The squad clings to opposite sides of the street, scanning the rooftops and windows through gun sights as they work their way toward the river. A machine gunner is posted at each intersection to provide backside security. Gradually, the troopers clear out critical buildings.

First the door is pounded on. If no one opens right away, the lock is blown off with a shotgun, or the door is blasted open with C4. Then each room is swept at riflepoint. Most structures seem empty, but some have young men or families in them, who are gathered up for relocation to a safer quadrant further back, and in some cases for questioning.

Nearby, booms and machine gun bursts can be heard as adjoining squads encounter fire. Thick smoke begins to rise in several parts of the neighborhood. At one point there is a loud exchange of automatic fire and grenades very close by. The soldier carrying the platoon's shotgun sidles up to me, holding it in an outstretched hand, his

M-4 hanging by his side. "Do you know how to use this?"

"Uh-huh."

"Well if this shit gets any hotter I'm gonna give it to you. You just look for me, pal."

SNIPER

We are starting to work along the Euphrates riverfront when the radio brings an order to secure access to a pontoon bridge which straddles the river nearby. The squad's machine gun is set up behind some sandbags along the embankment wall. The captain tells some soldiers to enter a building which is the highest on the block so they can climb onto its roof and establish a lookout.

They start to kick in the door when a quavery voice sings out in excellent English, "I am coming out! I'm a doctor at the hospital and I am coming out!" A very sweaty and shaky man in his mid-thirties steps forward with his hands up. "My family is inside." The squad brings out his wife, and three children between two and ten.

"Sir, the coalition forces need access to your house to secure this area," explains the captain. "Nothing will be touched, but you must leave the area now. Please gather some things."

A few minutes later, the family is standing on the sidewalk with bag in hand, and plans are being made to transport them to a holding area. Suddenly, automatic fire rings out from a building across the river. We dive for cover. The family is hustled behind a steel newsstand on the street corner.

A few minutes later the sniper begins shooting again. "Which window? Where's it coming from?" scream several officers. "Look for the muzzle flash!" Opposite us on the south bank is an entire block of four-story buildings, perhaps a hundred windows and myriad roofs where a gunman could set up. Every few minutes our invisible assailant lets loose again. We are pinned.

A message is radioed, and perhaps twenty minutes later we spot a platoon of soldiers from the 325th trotting down the south bank to surround the buildings opposite. They will search each floor. There is a lot of real estate to cover, and continued sporadic shooting keeps us mostly locked in place for the next two or three hours.

During this period, we get a radio warning that a busload of fedayeen were hustled into the neighborhood a little earlier. As we're digesting this, several vehicles try to rush the farther of the two bridges we are guarding. "What should I do?" screams the machine gunner. "Open up! Now!" Tracers from the .50 cal. and smoke trails from the RPG launcher arc perhaps two hundred meters to the bridge. A taxi and two small pickups keep rolling across and out of sight, with unknown effect on the occupants.

Elsewhere in the city, other technical vehicles are getting lit up this morning. As I watch from about three blocks away, two of the 82nd's Kiowas fly in low and hard, then pull up sharply in a kind of looping attack mode. They put missiles on two taxis being used by guerrillas, then one circles back for a second shot.

On another bridge, a propane truck that had been wired to blow tries to crash into U.S. troops. Fortunately, they shoot it into fiery oblivion part of the way over. In one of the weirdest attacks, a Bravo Company platoon working in the same neighborhood as the Bravo soldiers I ended up with spotted a man pushing an unusual wheelbarrow. This seemed odd in a war zone, so they went to check it out. As the wheelbarrow turned toward them, a man crouching inside opened up with an AK-47. Both guerrillas paid with their lives.

That same day, some guerrillas ambushed the supply convoy that I regularly rode back and forth between battalions, wounding four of the 82nd's soldiers. (Who in turn killed all ten Iraqis.) Sergeant Felipe Burgos, driving one of the trucks, was shot worst. The bullet just missed the supplemental hard plate on his body armor, and entered his chest. The soft portion of his armor slowed the round enough that it was deflected by a rib and narrowly avoided his heart, finally lodging near a kidney. Since it's too close to a major artery to risk removing it, he'll carry it there the rest of his life. Just the night before, Burgos had been joking that there was one medal he never wanted to win, and that was the Purple Heart. He'll have one anyway.

TEMPLATE FOR UP-RIVER?

The radio reports that Bravo's 3rd Platoon has found a huge ammo cache. Among many other types of ordnance it contains 2,000 boxes of AK-47 rounds. That's 200,000 bullets. They are eventually dumped into a deep waste-oil cistern in an industrial zone. (More often, newly discovered caches are exploded in place by the Army's EOD specialists, creating spectacular little mushroom clouds across the city throughout the day.) I later find out that the day's weapons haul also includes a number of ten-foot-long missiles, 450 RPGs, and 700 grenades.

Meanwhile, the Iraqi doctor whose house we commandeered has proven very personable and helpful. In speaking of the fedayeen he refers to them as "the criminals," and reports that they are mostly not locals but recent arrivals from either Baghdad or overseas seedbeds of Islamic fundamentalism. As the day passes, there are signs of support and even jubilation from some residents of the neighborhood. A large number of men gather under a covered arcade directly across the river from the bridge we are guarding, and many of them are waving and clapping, as well as pointing warning signs to certain buildings and windows.

Overall, the day is a great success. The heart of the city and the center of the fedayeen resistance have now been penetrated. Five uniformed Iraqi soldiers have been taken prisoner, plus one fedayeen thought to be Syrian.

And the raid produced only three U.S. casualties—all non-life-threatening wounds from mortar shrapnel. It will take the 82nd a while to fully pacify and stabilize Samawah, but with the Baath party's back broken, the local Shia population, which hates Saddam, is likely to do much of the final rooting out of local guerrillas.

In one week of fighting, the 82nd has liberated one of Iraq's major cities, with few innocent Iraqis killed, and relatively little damage done to the city's physical infrastructure (such as it is—most of Iraq was a ruin long before the war thanks to Saddam's dastardly misrule).

Most important, a military template has been established. While the Samawah fighting has been exhausting, dirty, and dangerous for the brave soldiers and pilots of the 82nd, the battle has come to fruition with considerably less bloodshed than in other Iraqi cities. The operation hasn't been nearly as deadly as either military history or basic logic would lead one to expect for a large urban sweep.

The remarkable fact is that, with the military phase of the campaign approaching its close, and the next phase of humanitarian relief about to kick into gear, only one American has lost his life in the liberation of Samawah. Less than twenty others from the 82nd Airborne have been wounded. If this dramatic success can be replicated by American forces in Baghdad, a priceless formula for avoiding nightmarish street casualties will have been discovered, and Americans and Iraqis alike will have reason to rejoice.

7

THE SACRED PROFANITY OF WAR

BASSAN

LATE AFTERNOON, APRIL 4—This is, however, a war. And war always includes tragedy.

The Iraqi doctor's house is searched for weapons or indications of Baath party connections. None are found, so it is decided to let him and his family remain in their home provided they promise to stay indoors and allow U.S. troops occasional access. The doctor agrees and the platoon splits, half remaining to guard the bridge, and half of us heading down an adjoining alley. We have traveled barely fifty meters when we stumble upon war's cruelest face.

A boy about ten years of age is lying on a soiled mattress pad in a hideous alley. He was caught in the morning's fighting, and his clothing, arms, legs, and face are soaked in blood. On every inch of his body the flies are so thick he looks more black than brown. Across his middle is a crude bandage. We shout for Doc, the platoon's medic, who comes at a run.

While I wave my arms to dislodge some of the flies, Doc cuts off the boy's clothes and the bandage, which was fashioned by a neighbor. What we see underneath is gruesome. A grotesque gash the size of a dinner plate has taken off much of the flesh on the boy's left side, from the hip up to his rib cage. His internal organs are visible through the gaping hole in his torso.

"Oh, man, this kid is hurt bad," Doc mutters, beads of sweat breaking out on his brow. He dons gloves and applies a large compress to the wound. I ask the neighbor the boy's name. It is Bassan.

Suddenly Bassan starts to wretch. His eyes roll. It looks like he is about to vomit. I expect a gory surge of regurgitated blood from internal bleeding. "Look at me Bassan," Doc says loudly, signaling the boy to keep eye contact. "I'm going to take care of you, but you have to stay calm and stay awake."

"This kid is shocking hard. He's gonna die soon if we can't get him somewhere better."

"The Iraqi doctor is just down the street," I blurt out.

"He said he works in the hospital. Maybe he can help."

"Get him. Fast," Doc orders.

Within minutes the doctor is kneeling in the alley. For fifteen minutes the American medic and Iraqi physician struggle to get an IV started. The child has had such a massive loss of blood, all of his veins have collapsed. Finally they get a bag of electrolytic fluid started in a vein of his foot.

The alley is strewn with rubbish, animal hair, food scraps, and excrement. A shallow V-shaped drainage channel down its center encloses a ribbon of vile, soupy liquid, much of it human waste poured out from adjoining homes. The muddy green trickle, but an arm's length from where Bassan lies, swarms with pestilential insects. I fan madly for half an hour in an attempt to drive away the horrid flies as they try to devour the poor child's bloody flesh.

The soldiers debate what can be done. Should the boy go to an Iraqi hospital? A U.S. aid station? How can he be gotten there? An American ambulance would have to have an armed escort to enter this neighborhood. It's too far to carry a litter. Eventually, an incredibly dilapidated fifteen-passenger minibus is commandeered from a neighbor. Will the Iraqi doctor come with us? "Of course."

Bassan is gently lifted into the vehicle, and a soldier drives it to the end of the alley, where it is met by two Delta Company gun trucks for the run to the temporary aid station set up by medics in a more secure location.

(Not entirely secure, however: soldiers man machine guns at each of the windows as the American medics work assiduously to treat Iraqi patients in the center of the building.)

There are no U.S. physicians here; this is only a first aid station. But it turns out our friend the Iraqi physician is a surgeon. "Could you operate right here, right now, to stanch the boy's internal bleeding?" asks one medic after a glance at the gaping hole.

The physician hesitates visibly. "Do you have anesthesia?"

"No. But we have morphine."

"Well, I am willing to try."

The thought is mind boggling. The aid station is in another filthy, dusty building. There is very little medical equipment, no running water at all. And the horrifying wound is now fouled with all sorts of contaminants.

During a quiet moment while radio calls are being made to see if a medevac helicopter can be located, I turn to the Iraqi doctor, with whom I have spent most of the day. I ask him his name. He measures me with a long pause. "What would you do with that information?"

"I am going to write about you in an American magazine."

"I'm sorry, but if I give my name and it becomes known to the authorities that I have been cooperating with Americans it will be very dangerous for me."

Even with five thousand American soldiers in his city, this Iraqi remains uncertain as to whether the Baath mafia are finally going to be driven out. I can tell from his comments throughout the day that he would welcome a regime change engineered by the United Sates, but he is unwilling to risk his life by committing to the American side until he is confident this will not be a replay of 1991, when the United States failed to finish off Saddam.

In a few minutes the decision is made to fly Bassan to a fully equipped American field hospital, where surgeons can try to save his life. It seems, frankly, a long shot. But the boy is tremendously brave. He never whimpers, and even smiles up at me a few times. I'll never forget his face.

This has been a wrenching twist in an overwhelming day.

THE EDGE OF CIVILIZATION

And Friday's drama was not yet done. The night would close for me with a tense four-truck convoy into the center of Samawah, where the battalion headquarters had been relocated for the night. Rifles poked from every window and truck opening as we rumbled along, much later in the evening than we had intended to remain out. I was riding atop a teetering pile of rucksacks in the back of a large, open stake truck.

The structure we would occupy that night was chosen because it was a sealed concrete tube with only two opposing openings that would need to be defended. Unfortunately, someone knew where we were. Just as the blacked-out convoy pulled up, we came under automatic weapons fire. An RPG whizzed through the night, detonating with a tremendous bang.

"Get out of the truck!" screamed the first sergeant at the driver and the five of us in back. I dove over the high wooden stakes that enclosed the cargo area. Unfortunately, the backpack I was wearing hung up on something. I was dangling about seven feet off the ground, like a fish flopping in the air at the end of a stringer.

I wriggled desperately but could not free myself. The firefight raged in the pitch black around me. After perhaps fifteen seconds that seemed like forever, I was able to rip my arms out of the straps. I fell to the ground heavily, leaving my pack snagged high on the truck. I limped into the tunnel, which we discovered was infested with rats the size of large guinea pigs. I lay down on some cardboard boxes to spend my last night in Iraq.

A few hours earlier that evening, I had had some time to reflect on events. After the all-night and then all-morning street combat in Samawah, and then the draining afternoon experience with Bassan, I had returned to the previous night's battalion headquarters, located at a sprawling abandoned cement plant. Whipped after thirty-three hours without sleep, I found an out-of-the-way office and lay down for a nap. By some sixth sense I awoke toward the end of daylight to an eerie silence.

I was alone in the building. The industrial ghost town which had been our staging grounds was suddenly almost entirely empty.

In war, improvisation is everything, and late in the afternoon a quick decision had been made to push the command post forward, right into the parts of the city fought over that day. Within hours of when the order was given, nearly everything had been whisked away by Army worker ants. I awoke as the decamping was nearly complete.

The astonishing access to events I was allowed while embedded with the 82nd had a flip side: I was responsible for my own fate. I found it possible to hustle my way into almost any battle, or planning session, or troop movement. But when I drifted off with some unit where I didn't have buddies, I knew there was no one keeping an eye out for me. That seemed fair enough. To report this story as I felt it should be, I needed that freedom, and I am not of the opinion that soldiers should have to babysit journalists. I was on my own, and knew it would be completely my fault if I got into a pinch.

As it happened, I wasn't quite left behind that evening. To my great relief, I discovered that a few soldiers remained on the premises, and that one last shift of four or five trucks would be returning to haul away the remainder of the command post equipment. When they finally rolled up, the prospect of an extra body and ruck-sack didn't thrill the testy, sleep-deprived grunts who were jamming the final six pounds of gear into their five-pound bag. But I would've jumped on a fender to avoid being stranded in this yawning industrial abyss, with hundreds of dark corners hard in the middle of Comanche territory.

Our wait for the final trucks was longer, and more strained, than anyone expected. For a few hours, a handful of other men and I milled about the vast industrial warren of the darkening cement plant. As the blackness deepened, the soldiers began to nervously scan alleys and rooftops, buckle their armor and helmets, and chamber rounds in their weapons. Sentries walked out into the gloom to cover corners.

The first sergeant tried to establish a radio check. "This is Red Falcon 3. Any unit on the net that can hear this, please relay." No answer. The truck had lost the time synch that secures military transmissions, or the frequency, or just line of sight. There was no radio contact. We paced uneasily as we awaited our promised mounts.

I eventually sat down next to a broken-down date palm tree, beside the chaplain—a Special Forces soldier who had retired, become a Catholic priest, then rejoined the Army as a padre. Perching somewhat incongruously on two decorous, matching white chairs that somebody had found and dragged outside, we scanned the dark outlines of the spooky twisted ruins. For perhaps twenty minutes we reclined wordlessly.

Overhead, the heavens remained crystalline. The moonless night before, I had navigated into warfare solely by the light of these stars. Now I soaked in their warm glint for a very different purpose. Over and over this month, those pure sparks had represented for me the principles that are true and unvarying in all places and at all times. They reassured me of the permanent beauty of God's world.

But down here on earth tonight, among man, all was broken, dirty, and smoke filled. Mangy inbred dogs, their stretched teats hanging in rows, pawed through decades of accumulated refuse. A stink of burning garbage filled our noses. Nearby, an AC-130 Specter began to circle, and then to rain down steel on some adjoining snakepit, the enormous cannon throbbing at us like an invisible metronome.

I was swept yet again with a feeling of the thinness of civilization. At this moment, fine concepts like justice and fairness and mercy, as well as life itself, were only as permanent as the handful of men and few weapons and machines that stood between us and blackness, filth, and cruelty. It is an almighty strain on the soldiers bearing the burden, but Americans need to be here—because a good world is made, not found. And good men who want to build something safe and decent amidst the blackness must find other good men they can rely on for support, mutual protection, and brotherly love.

My mind returned to the words of Psalm 144, as they had echoed around our pre-combat campfire just one long night earlier.

Blessed be the Lord, my rock,
who trains my hands for war,
and my fingers for battle;
my rock and my fortress,
my stronghold and my deliverer,
my shield, in whom I take refuge,
who subdues the peoples under me. . . .
Bow your heavens, O Lord, and come down;
touch the mountains so that they smoke.
Make the lightning flash and scatter them;
send out your arrows and rout them.
Stretch out your hand from on high;
set me free
and rescue me from the mighty waters,
from the hands of aliens,
whose mouths speak lies,
and whose right hands are false. . . .
May our sons in their youth
be like plants full grown,
our daughters like corner pillars,
cut for the building of a palace.
May our barns be filled,
with produce of every kind. . . .
May there be no breach in the walls,
no exile
and no cry of distress in our streets.

AFTERMATH

8

HOMECOMING

BLACK HAWK UP (C-130 OUT)

By the end of the first week of April, the military liberation of Samawah was complete. It had become clear to me that the U.S. military operation was nearly over. Baghdad was encircled and effectively under U.S. control. Iraq would be free within days.

By this point, I was pretty beaten up. My body and mind were badly sleep deprived. I'd lost fifteen pounds. Large bruises marked various limbs, and I had torn a thigh muscle in my frantic leap from the stake truck. It hit 105 degrees on my last day in Iraq and (like the soldiers I accompanied) I was filthy after weeks without a shower.

But I had a great story, which I needed to rush home to the American public. That, however, is not easily done in a combat zone. I would have to improvise and hustle to get back to the world of airliners and taxicabs and rental cars. And I knew that each of the first hops in my return to civilization might take days to arrange.

My first step was to get to brigade headquarters. Once again, my little trick of bumming rides on the food and water trucks got me moving. In fact, luck was on my side—the battalion I'd overnighted with was running unusually short of supplies, so the convoy trucks and their armed escorts left several hours earlier than the normal milk run.

Over the next two days, my luck got even better. Shortly after I arrived at the brigade HQ, two Black Hawk helicopters touched down. That got my antenna up. A casual conversation with the pilots revealed that they were carrying an American and Australian Special Forces team planning a mission in the area. Special Forces operatives are fiercely closemouthed and media shy. Several times in Iraq I was tempted to photograph an SF soldier (they are often ragged and unshaven to blend in with local populations) or one of their operational vehicles (beat-up civilian trucks they have hotwired, or special Humvees packed with gear—many of them bearing large NYPD stickers plastered to their windshields or bumpers). But I learned that shooting portraits of the SF was a good way to get a loud wrangle going.

I didn't ask any details about this mission, but I did learn from the pilots that in three hours both Black Hawks would be carrying the team back to Tallil Air Base. Could I possibly squeeze in with them? I delivered my full hearts-and-flowers pitch. Most pilots are good guys, relaxed about bureaucracy, and happy to share their steeds whenever possible. And they tend to be more media friendly than many soldiers. The answer was yes, they'd take me.

But I knew plans could change fast, and that there wasn't going to be any nice attendant making an announcement inviting lame reporters and other unarmed passengers to preboard along with families including small children. So I dragged my pack onto the pad right next to the choppers (putting it on at that point would be much too presumptuous), and then perched myself there on the concrete, ready to hop on the second they decided to fly. In the triple-digit heat and aching midday sun the hours dragged, but I stuck to those helicopters like a buzzard on a meatwagon.

I struggled to type on my laptop. Every reporter's worry when he takes on an assignment is that there won't be enough good material to produce a strong story. Here, I had exactly the opposite problem; my fingers couldn't move across the keyboard fast enough to keep up with the incredible things I was seeing. All day long,

I would scratch frantic notes on small pads of paper. Then, every moment I had some downtime, I would fire up my computer and start to translate these thoughts into a narrative. It was hard. Most of the time I would have to sit cross-legged in the dust, or in an empty vehicle, or leaning against a bumper or wheel. I'd spread out my notes, hope there would be no breeze, hope I had enough juice in my batteries, hope the accumulating sand and crud hadn't killed my computer, hope for enough momentary calm to let me write.

One persistent problem was simply that the dull glow of my laptop's screen was often almost impossible to see in the relentless Iraqi sun. I wrote at night as much as I could stay awake, and during the day I would seek the shade of vehicles, or a medical tent, or rig a hood stretching over my head and computer. This was suffocating, and rough on my back, but it allowed me to see what I had typed.

Suddenly, the SF guys and some accompanying soldiers appeared. The helicopter turbines began to wind, and I threw my bags on, keeping my head down in the hope no one would ask who the hell I was and where I thought I was going. Nobody said a word. I stuffed in my earplugs, we lifted off, and I said a quiet prayer of thanks. It was my first big break in getting these words quickly into print.

There were about eight of us jammed in tight on the open cargo floor of the Black Hawk. In a helicopter, unlike all other vehicles, a soldier rides with his weapon barrel pointed down, so that if there is an accidental discharge it goes through the floor. Nobody in a chopper wants anything to damage the rotor or turbine up overhead. The Aussie commando across from me was a cool character, his lanky 6'5" frame clad in Australia's distinctive yellow-brown desert camouflage, his eyes locked behind a pair of black Ray Bans. I wondered to myself: "Where the devil has he been living to be able to show up here at the end of the earth with that long, thick black hair improbably clean and unmussed?"

There was a din of noise and a percussive beating of wind. The hatches on both sides of the helicopter were open so the gunners could lean out, training their .50 calibers on each truck or knot of Iraqis as we flew over them low, ready to react at the first hostile muzzle flash. I stared out at the arid brown pancake that is south-central Iraq. The soldiers who were packed against my shoulders and legs shut their eyes and drowsed.

I wasn't invited to the SF party, so the chopper dropped me at a remote corner of the huge Tallil Air Base. This was a problem; I was miles from any identifiable helpmates. I started to hike. But the military kindness and combat-zone fraternity I experienced over and over kicked in almost instantly. Some soldiers passing by in a Humvee stopped to offer me a ride. Thanks to the consideration of a sergeant at their destination, this led to a second, longer ride which dumped me right next to the vast MiG bunker where my buddies in the 82nd's helicopter battalion had established their camp. I hadn't seen them in quite some time, so there were hearty greetings followed almost immediately by rushed good-byes. I was now at the major supply base for the American forces in Iraq, and the U.S. Air Force was running cargo in hard. I needed to talk my way onto something headed back empty.

Lieutenant Engelbrecht drove me over to the strip where the C-130 cargo planes came in. Providence was again on my side: Just as we rolled in, there was a plane winding up for a freight pickup in Kuwait City. Yet another cooperative serviceman gave me a wave, and ten minutes after arriving I walked up the bird's tail. The cargo ramp closed instantly behind me. I never had so much room to myself in an airplane; it's not likely I ever will again. It was all raw, riveted aluminum, but I lay down in the cavernous bay, exhausted, and slept my way back to the civilized world.

An hour after stepping onto the tarmac at Kuwait International I had a seat on a KC-10 aerial refueling plane headed to Ramstein Air Base in Germany. From there, I hitched one more ride to McGuire Air Force Base in central New Jersey. These last two legs were my hardest—the closer I got to modernity, the more the military bureaucracy kicked in. "Where are your orders? What's your manifest number? You can't get there from here." But I was lucky: The cargo flow surging from the Western world to the Middle East at that moment was enormous. Planes were being requisitioned from all over the globe to take part in one of the heaviest airlifts in history. Those flying trucks bringing in ammo, food, soldiers, vehicles, and supplies were deadheading back in the direction that I needed to go, almost all of them empty, so the sheer numbers were on my side. By the time I walked off the last leg of my trip—a US Airways commercial flight bridging from Philadelphia to New York—it was just forty-three hours after I had climbed onto a water truck in an Iraqi war zone. A miraculous migration.

SNOW THERAPY

My first days back in the United States, I felt possessed. Deeply moved by what I had witnessed, I desperately wanted to rise to the occasion, to find the right words to capture the remarkable work I had observed from so many dutiful soldiers. In the middle of many nights I rose with some memory or image stuck in my head, climbed the stairs to my third-floor study, and began to write or rewrite.

I was also having a hard time putting the cityscapes and deserts of Iraq behind me. Several times in the first couple of weeks I snapped suddenly from sleep with all my synapses firing at full alert: Where am I? Where's my helmet? Do I dare lift my head safely here? As I foggily realized I was in my own home, I would begin to chuckle, then sometimes nearly cry, at my own dream-state lunacy.

My first week back was a kind of mirror image of the rich week before I left. I live outside Syracuse, New York, and am a lifelong fan of the Syracuse University sports teams. My sixteen-year-old son, an athlete himself, likewise dotes on the Orangemen—with the existential intensity that only a teenaged male can rouse up. Readers who are sports fans know that SU stormed through the NCAA college basketball tournament during March and early April of 2003, while I was in Iraq. The night after I returned to the United States, Syracuse played in—and won—the national championship. I don't need to tell you it meant a lot to my son and me to share that emotional climax.

That very same weekend, our friends in the Syracuse Symphony played a triumphant concert at Carnegie Hall in New York City. A day or two later, my younger son had a "public speaking night" where he and other third-grade classmates delivered wonderful speeches they had carefully prepared and honed—yet another family milestone I was very glad not to have missed. About the same time, my ninth-grade daughter won high honors in a classical piano competition. My family life went from zero to sixty in about three seconds.

These were very personal events, obviously. I mention them because, like the daily incidents I sketched at the very beginning of this book, they reminded me in heart-grabbing ways how intensely rewarding everyday life in our nation can be. American society abounds with opportunities for individuals to soar, and I felt that deeply during my homecoming, in many practical ways.

It wasn't very many days before I had finished a first draft of my manuscript and sorted all my photos. I rammed out an installment of the magazine I run, bringing subscribers direct-from-the-front dispatches practically while the dust was still settling from the events described. I did more than a dozen talk-radio interviews to promote the issue. Then I collapsed.

As a sixth-generation resident of snow country, I love winter. When I left for Iraq, we were skiing and building forts and cocooning at home amidst glorious white. When I returned, there was still ice on the lake, but the snow had all disappeared. Somehow, I felt cheated of my full measure of brisk weather. The fact that I'd been sojourning in the Godforsaken heat and sand of the Middle East only heightened my sense of having missed something from winter.

As my lungs now filled with sweet moist air, and my eyes soaked up the greenness of central New York, I swore to myself I would never again complain about fifty degree weather and plant-nourishing rain. And it will be a long time before I ever voluntarily set my foot on a baking beach! Instead, I found myself craving a chance to unwind with my family amidst the clean crispness of snow and mountains. When I proposed driving to Canada to seek out some iciness, my wife—who had just been through a dinger of a winter in its entirety—looked at me like I was crazy. (Was this the first sign of post-traumatic stress disorder?) Other relatives warned against going to Canada because the SARS epidemic was just then erupting there. At that particular moment, though, SARS exposure didn't seem such a grave risk to me.

After I explained the sources of my snow hunger, my good family indulged me. Soon we were driving under beautiful blue skies along the mighty St. Lawrence River, past the white clapboard house that constituted the rural border crossing of our extraordinarily friendly and open nation, and then on up to Mont Tremblant, in the Laurentian Mountains north of Montreal. Brisk astringent air, alpine rock, clean snow, Quebec country food, and swooshing family ski runs proved the perfect antidote to the broiling drear of Iraq.

On our way back through Montreal we attended a moving nighttime Easter vigil at the Church of Canada's Christ Church Cathedral. The next morning we returned for the Easter service. The glorious pageant of music and celebration screeched to a halt for me, however, when Archbishop Andrew Hutchison ladled out an unexpected dose of anti-Americanism in his homily. In his second paragraph he moaned that:

> The land in which the faith journeys of the three great monotheistic religions began is occupied by an invading Army, the treasures of an ancient civilization have been ravaged, thousands of innocent civilians and combatants

are dead and maimed, and the whole region is in political uproar. The dark shadow of fear creeps over much of the world as we try to imagine the consequences of what is now set in motion.

I was sitting with my family in the very front row of the cathedral, and it was all I could do to stifle myself from standing up amongst the hundreds gathered there—my hair a military stubble and my skin turned a leathery brown by the Iraqi sun—and replying, "Reverend, I'm sorry but you're wrong, wrong, wrong on every count."

INNOCENTS SPARED

Let's begin with this idea that American soldiers killed "thousands of innocent civilians and combatants." The gentleness of the U.S. military effort that had struck me repeatedly on various battlefields was confirmed by my study of the wider war after I returned. The elaborate efforts to avoid collateral bombing damage, the strict rules of engagement that prohibited firing unless fired upon, the extraordinary voluntary restraint shown by thousands of soldiers and Marines, the protection of mosques, schools, and historical monuments—these actions were amply documented.

I'm not the only journalist to describe such cases;

many international reporters accompanying troops throughout the war zone told similar stories. "I witnessed Iraqi paramilitary troops using women and children as human shields, turning grade schools into fortresses, and defiling their own holy sites. Time and again, I saw Americans taking unnecessary risks to clear buildings without firing or using grenades, because it might injure civilians. I stood in awe as nineteen-year-olds refused to return enemy fire because it was coming from a mosque," wrote *Time* magazine correspondent Jim Lacey, a fellow embedded journalist.

This reality ought to have been obvious to every serious observer of the Iraq conflict. And anyone with even fragmentary knowledge of the way battles are normally conducted will recognize that the liberation of Iraq stands as a momentous departure in war, a remarkable and welcome aberration from the bloodiness of most military operations. Even a liberal cleric in a nation experiencing an irrational spasm of anti-Americanism should not be blind to this.

There is not now, and probably never will be, a widely accepted count of Iraqis killed in the spring of 2003, but the best figures available suggest that perhaps two thousand or three thousand civilians died in the process of U.S. liberation of that large nation (and some of these were killed by fellow Iraqis). This despite the fact that the gangsters in control insisted on fighting from hospitals, taxis, religious shrines, and residential districts.

Recall that more than 3,200 Americans were killed in

a single day on September 11. Recall that Saddam killed more than 100,000 Iraqis in the months after the first Gulf War just to solidify his grip on power. Despite the individual tragedy behind every death, the loss of so few Iraqis in 2003 in the process of ridding their country of tyranny represents a blessedly low level of collateral damage.

And those light losses were no accident, but rather the end result of repeated difficult choices by U.S. commanders and GIs. Over and over, our warfighters went out of their way to spare the innocent while destroying the murderous, even when this allowed Iraqi fighters to escape, or exposed U.S. forces to greater personal danger.

Fortunately, casualties among American troops were also comparatively light. At this writing, nearly two months after the end of major combat, 196 U.S. soldiers have been killed in Iraq. That figure is stunningly low in comparison to other wars. The first Gulf War, for instance, which accomplished far less, brought 293 U.S. deaths. Among the 82nd Airborne there was, amazingly, just one fatality this time around. (A couple more U.S. soldiers in units attached to the 82nd also died.) More than thirty paratroopers were wounded in action, a few of them very seriously, and are now recovering.

I have just done an analysis of total U.S. fatalities by state, and find that, in general, our combat sacrifices were spread remarkably evenly across the Union, with most states suffering losses roughly in proportion to their share of the national population. States offering up somewhat more than their share of sons include Alabama, Arizona, Colorado, Delaware, Indiana, Maine, Michigan, Mississippi, Nevada, Oregon, Utah, Vermont, Virginia, and Wyoming. States with proportionally low contributions include Arkansas, Kentucky, Minnesota, Washington, and Wisconsin. The region that lost by far the most soldiers as a proportion of its total population was the West. States making up the Northeast/New England collective had casualties right in line with their population levels, as did the collective states of the South. The Midwest had proportionately low losses. One should avoid reading too much into these results, though, because with so few casualties in total, the differences between many states were just a soldier or two.

In any case, the surgical nature of America's sweep through Iraq was certainly noticed by the Iraqi people. In numerous places we saw Iraqis (sometimes whole families) standing by and watching attacks on individual government buildings, knowing that because of precise and careful U.S. targeting there was little reason to be afraid. The day before and the day after the fall of Baghdad, residents of the capital city were able to be out shopping, driving, and living comparatively normal lives—certainly not history's norm for an urban takeover.

When I was on combat patrols with soldiers, I saw Iraqis wave and smile. More significant, I saw them miming danger and pointing out the windows from which snipers were firing, putting themselves at risk to aid Americans battling Saddam. I met locals who expressed gratitude that the Baathist rogues had been killed with minimal destruction of civilian homes and infrastructure. This care won the United States goodwill from Iraqis (if not from Western opponents of the war), and will speed the postwar rebuilding of the country.

MISSING THE STORY

Another egregious error of the Montreal archbishop (whom I cite as a kind of proxy for other war critics) was his claim that, amidst the arrival of "an invading Army, the treasures of an ancient civilization have been ravaged." First of all, the worst predations against Iraq's historic treasures were carried out by the very government American soldiers went to Iraq to unseat. Over many years, Saddam and his cronies secretly removed Babylonian artifacts from museums and sold them abroad for personal cash, melted down ancient metalworks for their gold, and systematically neglected and abused archeological sites (like the Ziggurat of Ur which I gazed upon sadly across the wreckage of Tallil Air Base).

But the archbishop's slander grew out of bad information provided by others. Some of the most hysterical reporting of the entire Iraq War—subsequently echoed, re-echoed, and re-re-echoed by critics all around the globe—centered around the looting of the Iraqi National

Museum in Baghdad. The initial reports stated that thousands of priceless and irreplaceable artifacts had disappeared, many likely never to be seen again.

The stories gushed out when low-level museum employees entered the building after American forces liberated Baghdad, saw empty cabinets and shelves, and shrieked to drama-seeking foreign reporters that all the best pieces were gone—apparently taken by the looters who went on a spree the moment Saddam's enforcers disappeared from the scene. Western critics howled, academics resigned positions in protest, and opportunists attacked the "barbarism" of U.S. forces for failing to better secure the museum. Swept up in the rumors, many Iraqis assumed that U.S. troops stole the valuable artifacts. And a fresh wave of anti-American indignation rippled through Europe.

But the reporting that sparked all this storm and fury was wrong. Completely wrong.

Yes, the cabinets were empty. *But that's because the museum's senior employees had stashed all the really valuable parts of the collection in vaults just as fighting broke out.* "We knew a war was coming, so it was our duty to protect everything," explained a museum director.

Alas, only one reporter in Baghdad bothered to check beneath the surface of the juicy treasure-looting story for the real facts. By talking to museum official Donny George, Yaroslav Trofimov of the *Wall Street Journal* managed, rather easily, to discover the unreported truth. By the time Trofimov's revelation was printed on April

17, though, the reporting frenzy had proceeded so far that the international public had become irrevocably convinced that the national treasures of Iraq had all been hauled away by vandals. And the media did very little to correct the record subsequently. At the time I write, the number of items thought to be missing from the museum has been revised from the original, blindly reported claim of 170,000 (what kind of writer would print a number like that without skepticism?) all the way down to 25 artifacts, none of them particularly consequential. Yet I dare say most readers of this book will be learning for the first time from my account that the museum-looting story was almost entirely bogus.

And the media was guilty of more than just reporting unchecked information and then rumor-mongering that falsehood into an artificial scandal. There was an accusatory tone to much of this reporting right from the beginning. Why are American soldiers blamed if Iraqi yahoos decide to go wilding the day after they throw off Saddam's thirty-year yoke?

There was no intelligent differentiation in the reporting between the several varieties of looting: righteously outraged citizens plundering Saddam's palaces and government offices (political behavior); scavenging by desperately poor people long denied life's very basics while the oligarchs among them luxuriated (survival instinct); thefts from museums, libraries, and banks that included some inside jobs carried out by Baath party bosses with keys; simple criminal activity; and everyday post-Super-

Bowl-style anarchy. And in all these cases, media castigation unfortunately tended to be directed not at the Iraqi perpetrators, but at American troops for "not doing enough" to stop them.

This blame-casting conveniently ignored a host of practical problems faced by our soldiers. My favorite illustration of this is supplied by my fellow embedded journalist Jonathan Foreman of the *New York Post*. He describes watching an AP reporter in a car pull up to an American soldier. The reporter had just noticed that the Iraqi Ministry of Information, where she was heading for her daily dose of fantasy, was in flames. "Why aren't you putting out the fire?" the reporter demanded angrily of Sergeant William Moore of the Army's 3rd Infantry Division—overlooking little details like the fact that there were no hydrants, no hoses, no pumper trucks, and no working water lines in Baghdad. "How the hell am I supposed to do that?" responded the astonished Sergeant Moore. Turning away, he muttered, "Piss on it?"

This tendency to blame American GIs first—most prominent among reporters and others safely ensconced far from where the bullets were flying—surfaced numerous times during the war. There was the criticism of U.S. officers for their "failure" to stop Iraqis from breaking into the national library. But this failure to intervene was no casual dereliction. It was a battlefield decision taken to avoid casualties and the destructive fire of weapons into a sensitive site. Once again, the *Wall Street Journal* was the only media outlet in Baghdad enterprising enough to discover the truth. As the *Journal* eventually reported, Lieutenant Colonel Eric Schwartz of the U.S. Army's 3rd Infantry Division's Task Force 1-64, "whose functions also include feeding the lions in the abandoned Baghdad Zoo next door, couldn't move into the museum compound and protect it from looters because his soldiers were taking fire from the building—and were determined not to respond."

It didn't occur to the anchormen and sniffing Western curators who, from their snug offices, casually excoriated U.S. troops for not saving more manuscripts and artifacts that doing so would have required ending a good number of equally priceless Iraqi and American lives, and very likely done even more physical damage to the building and its contents. Can you imagine the reaction of these very same critics if the United States *had* used force to secure the structure and killed Iraqis and damaged collections in the process?

THE ROOTS OF MEDIA MALPRACTICE

One must ask where the negativity that colored this story from its inception came from. The answer is: from the inchoate antimilitary suspicion that is permanently in the air in most editorial suites. I ran up against some of this myself when I filed reports from Iraq. There was, for instance, a story I sent to the *Los Angeles Times* describing certain of my interactions with Colonel Bray, whom I characterized as an impressive leader of infantrymen. An editor back in L.A. refused to run the article without inserting a sentence at the end warning that this positive assessment may have been influenced by the fact that I was embedded with U.S. troops myself, and therefore perhaps too sympathetic to their point of view. I was unreachable in the desert after sending the report in, and knew nothing of this outrageous attempt at backseat editorializing. Thankfully, my magazine staff fought on my behalf and managed to get the offensive disclaimer watered down to a relatively innocent half-sentence attached to my conclusion: "Those who claim that 'embeds' have fallen under the mystique of the military may dismiss my view, but this man I see before me is very much a leader rather than a ruler."

For the record, my views of the U.S. military's performance in Iraq were formed by nothing but close daily scrutiny of their operations. The embedding experience was just a large-scale version of what I do for a living: I inveigle myself into some profession, or city, or corporation, or government agency, carefully study how the people there operate, and then describe in terms understandable to a layman what it is that's interesting or important about what goes on in that place. I've perpetrated my craft from the oil fields of Alaska, from Wall Street, from the back seat of police cruisers, from Israel's West Bank, from Nashville studios and churches, and in many other places. And I have to say that I have never been given as much freedom to explore and talk to people without restriction, so many chances to see sensitive information and procedures, so many open doors, and so many shoulders to peer over as the U.S. military allowed me during the Iraq War.

I was on no leash. I went wherever I wanted without handlers (the Army public affairs officers rarely even knew where I was). I talked to everybody, from major general to machine gunner to military dentist. Every reasonable request for information was satisfied.

The unprecedented embedding program launched by the Pentagon during this war was an enormous risk. If there had been any serious slipups, there would have been scribes all over them, up close and personal, with no chance to sweep anything away or airbrush the details. I can assure you that the *New York Times*, CNN, ABC, and *Newsweek* are not about to let any similarly snoopy observers into *their* boardrooms or staff offices during some equivalent period of crisis operation. This reflects the U.S. military's confidence in the righteousness of their work, the competence of their leadership, and the professionalism of their rank and file. I am full of admiration for the people who took this risk, and—I freely admit—impressed that we have a military this open.

And I am quite certain I'm more qualified to pass objective judgment on these soldiers than some newsroom spinner who has carefully avoided "bias" by never in his life spending any time actually observing military folks in action. I find it sad that James Poniewozik of

Time magazine would criticize the embedded journalists as "biased," scalding us for spotlighting the swiftness and sureness with which American forces crushed the ballyhooed Republican Guards. It is pitiful, and disturbing, that John MacArthur, the trust-fund baby who uses grandpa's money to publish *Harper's* magazine, would brand both the embedded media and the U.S. military as "propagandists" for the Bush reelection campaign. What the hell does he know about what really happened in Baghdad and points south?

A classic example of a media figure abusing his access to national microphones to rave in unobjective ways against war was the commencement address given at Rockford College in May by *New York Times* reporter Chris Hedges. He described the U.S. unseating of Saddam as a grab for "empire" that showed us to be "pariahs, tyrants to others weaker than ourselves." He charged that "the only two ministries we bothered protecting" in Baghdad were "the oil ministry and the interior ministry"—presumably because America came to Iraq "for oil and occupation."

On and on Hedges thundered: "We do not understand . . . ," "We bumbled in . . . ," "It will be a cesspool . . . ," "Damaging to our souls . . . ," "We have blundered. . . ." Suggesting America has lost sight of "our own capacity for atrocity—for evil," Hedges argued that, yes, this was now a war of liberation: "A war of liberation by Iraqis from American occupation." (His middle-American audience of Illinois students and family members turned their backs, catcalled, and walked out during the address.)

This is appallingly ideological, overinflated rhetoric from a daily reporter of America's self-styled newspaper of record. Alas, it is the sort of thing one encounters very often in the offices and overseas hotel rooms of our media elites. Again, the roots are cultural. Hedges is a committed leftist who says he grew up admiring the communists in the Spanish Civil War and "wanted that epic battle to define my own life." He proudly describes being raised by a pacifist father who "took us as children to antiwar demonstrations," mocked soldiers, and insisted that war is always an "abomination." "If we visited museums, he would never allow us to see the displays of weapons." Both parents "were social activists," and his father "was very involved in the gay rights movement." All of which is fine in our nation where people are free to believe whatever they damn well please. But is this the right man to be objectively interpreting America's defense and foreign policies in the pages of the *New York Times*, *Dallas Morning News*, and other publications where he was entrusted with critical reporting? Is it reasonable that this man was given a Pulitzer Prize for war coverage?

Shortly after I returned stateside, Joel Kotkin and Fred Siegel, two wise observers of American culture (and lifelong Democrats) who closely followed the media war coverage on the home front (as I was obviously not able to do while in the thick of things) wrote a review in the *Weekly Standard* pronouncing "the prestige media" to be "big-time losers" in the second Gulf war:

The mission of the media is to provide accurate information. Yet for much of the war—indeed until the Army and Marines broke into Baghdad—the *New York Times* was often as full of misinformation as the Iraqi minister of information. And not nearly as funny.

It was indeed painful to see that despite rapid advances through the desert and the remarkable steps to avoid civilian casualties, the BBC and CNN tried to portray the invasion as a disaster in the making, or an "acid flashback to Vietnam," as the unintentionally amusing [*New York Times* columnist] Maureen Dowd put it. A typical experience was to hear left-wing dinosaur and onetime North Korea apologist Robert Scheer tell us on National Public Radio that immigrants—widely honored for their service—had served as "cannon fodder" for an imperial war.

We wonder how well his comments would play, say, on Whittier Boulevard in Latino East L.A., where there are more American flags flying than in Santa Monica. . . . For people like

Scheer, America's triumph, and the liberation of Iraq, was all about the agony of defeat, notably theirs. [Not] accuracy.

There is considerable evidence that inaccurate and slanted reporting has damaged the media's standing with the American public. Asked in late March, during the fighting's peak, how much confidence they had "that the press is giving an accurate picture of how the [Iraq] war is going," only 30 percent of Americans polled by the Pew Research Center answered "a great deal of confidence." That is lower than the 40 percent who said they had "a great deal of confidence" that the U.S. military "is giving the public an accurate picture of how the war is going." When the supposedly neutral observers in the press corps are getting much lower marks for objectivity than the special interest whose performance they are examining, the press has a problem.

The credibility of our major media has nose-dived over the last generation. Consider some data from Gallup, Harris, and Princeton Survey Research:

- By 58 to 39 percent, Americans think today's news organizations are more inaccurate than accurate. (That ratio was almost exactly reversed eighteen years ago.)

- Only 31 percent of the public now say the news media "help society to solve problems;" fully 58 percent feel reporters "get in the way of society solving problems."

- Only 30 percent believe news organizations "care about the people they report on;" 55 percent say "they don't care."

- Just 23 percent of our citizenry say the news media are "willing to admit mistakes;" a troubling 67 percent say our news reporters "try to cover up mistakes."

- Fully 72 percent of Americans now say "the news media has too much power and influence in Washington."

One of the ways the public is responding to all of this is by walking away: Nightly network news viewing fell from 58 percent at the beginning of the 1990s to 32 percent in 2002. During that same period, newspaper readership tumbled from 54 percent to 41 percent, public opinion specialist Karlyn Bowman points out. Americans believe our news media is out of balance—in reporting on the military, as well as other areas—and they object. How have we gotten into this state?

As Joel Kotkin has warned elsewhere, today's media is a caste—a highly inbred, insular, self-referential group, largely Ivy League, urban, and politically homogeneous, that lacks connection with many traditional American institutions and values. Reading his and Siegel's commentary brought me back to my observations, formed in the media-saturated camps in Kuwait, of the cultural gap separating the media from our military. And that gap, I'm afraid, reflects a more general divide which yawns between our military and the nation's liberal elites as a whole.

Out in the real America, citizens feel pretty closely intertwined with the U.S. armed forces. The little church I attend in our rural New York village of two thousand people had nineteen relatives and neighbors on the prayer list all through March and April because they were serving with our military in the Iraq theater. But in the typical graduating class of an Ivy League university today, there are no more than three or four individuals who enter military service. On many college campuses, ROTC continues to be banned. The number of congressmen with military records is at an all-time low, and the number of congressmen with children in the armed forces can be counted on one hand. Very few top journalists personally know *anyone* in the military, much less anything accurate about military work.

Too many American professionals exhibit an ugly sense of superiority toward the military. In his new book *Keeping Faith*, author Frank Schaeffer describes how, after sending other children to New York University and Georgetown, his affluent Boston neighbors expressed disappointment at his son's decision to become a Marine. "He's so bright and talented and could do anything!" blurted one man. "What a waste!"

In his Illinois speech, *New York Times* reporter Chris Hedges betrayed his outrageous bias by repeating exactly this kind of misinformation. He described American soldiers as "poor kids from Mississippi or Alabama or Texas who could not get a decent job or health insurance and joined the Army because it was all we offered them." What a scandalous misrepresentation of the fighting men and women I encountered in Iraq! And one built entirely on that reporter's unwitting sense of superiority to people serving in the military.

In at least one case, it appears a nose-thumbing haughtiness toward soldiers got journalists killed in Iraq. Earlier in this story I mentioned how upset some of my fellow journalists were when a television crew perished near Az Zubayr very early in the hostilities. When more details of this incident were reported after I returned home, it became clear to me that these were needless deaths brought on by the disdain of these reporters for both the realities of war and the counsel of military professionals.

Openly defying repeated warnings from U.S. Marines, the three European journalists and a translator raced two SUVs into Iraq on the second day of the war, without military knowledge or cooperation. A general ignorance of things martial prevented the TV crew from differentiating friendly and hostile forces as they encountered them, and from understanding how a battle might progress and when a fire zone might become safe. Their foolhardiness extended to a refusal to wear any body armor or helmets, and to strapping gas cans on the roof of their vehicles. Very soon these men were overrun by some Iraqi fighters, who commandeered their trucks to mount an attack on the Marines. The journalists were machine gunned, and one of their SUVs was incinerated when the roof-mounted gas cans burst into flames.

Nearly every one of these fatal decisions was ultimately built, I suggest, on a cavalier attitude toward military authority and judgment. The one reporter of the four who survived, a Belgian named Daniel Demoustier, expresses no regrets over the incident, telling another reporter in May, "It's absolutely necessary that we keep doing these things. I don't want to go with the military. I don't want to be controlled." Yet it wasn't just the reporters who paid for their misjudgments. Two U.S. Marines ordered to investigate the incident were also shot by Iraqi fighters.

9

LESSONS

AFTERSHOCKS

After the major combat had ended, and I was back in
the States, the 82nd got involved in a few high-profile
police actions in Iraq. In mid-April, infantrymen from
the division were based in and around Karbala, and 3rd
Battalion patrols uncovered an enormous ammunition
stash on the outskirts of the city that contained millions
of rounds. Officers said the ammunition was enough to
arm two full divisions, and more than most of them had
ever seen in their lives.

Other troopers from the 3rd Battalion investigated a compound on the north side of the city used by the Iraqi intelligence service. Local civilians told them that thousands of people had been tortured and killed there, and that there is a mass grave under one of the compound's main buildings. They showed the troopers hollow floors and partitions in the cellar, which they said sealed in bodies. Men who had been imprisoned in the complex pointed out ceiling hooks from which they had been hung, while bound, during interrogations.

The 82nd was still in Karbala, and nearby Najaf, in the third week of April when a million Shiite pilgrims descended on the two holy cities for the first time since Saddam Hussein had repressed their annual rite decades earlier. The strong impression of the news coverage back in the United States was that these people were unfriendly to the United States. Attempts by some Shiite clergy based in Iran to foment anti-Americanism among the travelers were emphasized, and photos of a few fanatics who cut themselves with swords in a bloody fervor were heavily reprinted in newspapers. Yet the truth is, the pilgrimage not only came off without conflict, it turned out to be a festive event that included many expressions of warmth and gratitude toward U.S. troops.

"Our headquarters compound was right on the main road that all the pilgrims walked down," Captain Robin Brown of the 82nd's helicopter battalion tells me. "So for three solid days there was this constant river of people, and they were singing, honking horns, celebrating. We would watch over the low wall, and people would wave to us, laugh, and smile."

"That was Easter weekend," she continues, "and I attended a sunrise service for the troops. At the end of the service we were sitting there receiving communion. There were large wooden crosses erected above us for the service, and just off to the side all these Shiite Muslims were streaming by, and everyone was looking at each other, and it was an amazingly festive, peaceful, joyful experience."

The captain notes that here and in many other places where she met Iraqis, she observed no anti-American feeling, and indeed much positive response. "We had a lot of contact with everyday people who were very pro-American. People would come up to us, kids would cheer. One time, near Najaf, some locals brought us a whole case of ice cold orange soda. I don't know where they got it, but we were thrilled to have our first cold drinks in months."

At the time of our conversation at the end of May, Brown had been back in the United States for about a week and a half, and expressed surprise that much of the news from Iraq was portraying a hostility toward Americans. At a loss to square this with her own experience, she hypothesized that "Maybe the mood changed really fast. Maybe once they realized democracy was coming they decided to jump in with complaints and chafing." I said that when I had returned home I noticed a similar disjunction between my own recent impressions and the news analyses, and I suggested to the captain that the real problem might be unrepresentatively gloomy reporting.

That's not to say that Iraq was friction-free during the 82nd's time there. A week after the Shiite pilgrimage, soldiers from the division's 1st Battalion got involved in the war's single deadliest encounter with civilian protesters. A group of about two hundred people in the city of Fallujah, a Baath party stronghold and pro-Saddam hotbed, besieged a school where the 82nd's soldiers were encamped. They were pressing a variety of real and imagined grievances (like complaints that troopers were somehow using their night-vision goggles to see through women's robes). At about 10:30 P.M. on April 28 firing broke out, and in this skirmish and another two days later, around fifteen Iraqis were killed.

The crowd was throwing rocks, and U.S. soldiers reported that some Iraqis began firing AK-47s into the school and at an American convoy. "We saw three guys on the roof firing into our building. Everybody could see the muzzle flashes," said Sergeant Nkosi Campbell. Worried about the rules of engagement, Campbell's men asked for, and received, permission to return fire. I am informed by Captain Roger Davis, the commander of the troops present (Charlie Company of the 1st Battalion), that soldiers in another part of the compound likewise asked their supervising officer, Sergeant Miller, for permission before returning fire.

Some Iraqis told reporters that the U.S. soldiers opened fire without provocation. That would be completely out of character with anything I observed in my time with these same men. In all interactions I witnessed where troublemakers were mixed in with civilian crowds, paratroopers strictly understood that they were to fire only if they were attacked by Iraqis who clearly had weapons.

My own experiences were wholly in accord with this account of an Iraqi-U.S. confrontation described by *Time* magazine correspondent Jim Lacey:

In one particular tense moment, a company of U.S. soldiers was preparing to guard the Mosque of Ali—one of the most sacred Muslim sites—when agitators in what had been a friendly crowd started shouting that they were going to storm the mosque. In an instant, the Iraqis began to chant and a riot seemed imminent. A couple of nervous soldiers slid their weapons into fire mode, and I thought we were only moments away from a slaughter. These soldiers had just fought an all-night battle. They were exhausted, tense, and prepared to crush any riot with violence of their own. But they were also professionals, and so, when their battalion commander, Chris Hughes, ordered them to take a knee, point their weapons to the ground, and start smiling, that is exactly what they did. Calm returned. By placing his men in the most non-threatening posture possible, Hughes had sapped the crowd of its aggression. Quick thinking and iron discipline had reversed an ugly situation and averted disaster.

As I polished my manuscript amidst the death throes of the Baath regime, and observed these aftershocks of the war, a number of conclusions leapt at me. In many ways, I realized, the 82nd's warfighting efforts in Iraq represented a perfect microcosm of the larger U.S. military campaign staged across that country. The 82nd's two stocks in trade—quick response, and close coordination with different branches of the military—were the signature occurrences of this war.

It was a stunningly short twenty-six days from the first crossing of the Kuwait border to the pacification of Tikrit. In less time than it takes a monthly magazine to get out a new issue, a territory bigger than the entire northeastern region of the United States had been pacified. This was accomplished by a multipronged force of U.S. air, armor, cavalry, and infantry working together across normal service boundaries. To accomplish this they relied on racing speed, superior technology, and overflowing stamina and courage among rank-and-file servicemen.

This lightning victory in Iraq confounded many naysayers. On the right, it shut up the depressives who insist American youth have all gone soft, no longer know how to sacrifice, and won't stand up for their nation. And on the left, a whole horde of nervous Nellies and faithless critics who were certain our troops would "bog down" in a "quagmire" ended up looking like fools.

I suspect much of today's drumbeat about America's "failure" to bring instant recovery to Iraq, and the alleged impossibility of introducing that nation to political and economic modernity, will also look pretty foolish not too far down the road. The critics need to have some faith in the Iraqi people, show a little patience with the military and civilian administrators just now beginning their jobs, and stop blowing minor complaints from each Iraqi extremist-faction-of-the-week into a full-fledged indictment of America's stabilizing presence.

On the whole, I myself am relatively optimistic about Iraq's prospects. The country has nowhere to go but up. I have traveled and worked in some of the poorest societies in the world, in Africa, Latin America, and central Asia, but none struck me as more wretched and dislocated than Iraq. Walking its land and streets, I was appalled at how decayed the country has become. Dense networks of canals and dikes—which once must have made the desert bloom throughout central Iraq—have obviously been in disrepair for many years. The cities I saw were a mess—without effective sewage, water, telephone, power, or transport systems. Most vehicles were broken down. During Saddam's reign, per capita incomes in Iraq fell to one-tenth their previous levels, and schools have closed all across the nation.

But Iraq, unlike Afghanistan, is not a fundamentally ignorant and premodern country. As I've mentioned, it was the center of learning for the Arab world just a generation ago. There are still many highly skilled individuals in the country, including some who spoke beautiful English with me. And of course Iraq sits on top of the second most valuable store of petroleum on the planet.

This is not a land bereft of opportunities. To the contrary, it is a nation unusually well endowed with natural and human resources. Its problem is fairly simple: It has been one of the worst governed places on earth during current lifetimes. Remember those twenty-three separate coups since 1920, capped by Saddam's insane tinhorn despotism.

All of this makes it a reasonable prospect that Iraq, given some firm oversight from the U.S., could shoot into a dramatically improved condition over the next decade. And if a core of tolerably just and prosperous nations takes root around the Persian Gulf—with Kuwait, Qatar, Dubai, Bahrain, and other Gulf States well on the way, Iraq headed down the right path, and Iran likely next in line—the perenially ugly prospects of the Middle East could evolve in a heartening and unexpectedly positive direction during the first decade of the twenty-first century. That is at least now a fairly rational bet.

Anyone with a sense of history, and an appreciation of human tragedy, would have to consider that possibility one of the most welcome developments of our generation. An unbloodied Middle East would make the entire globe a safer and more prosperous place. It is certainly a hope worth taking some risks on behalf of—even though it will put the United States in the unfamiliar position of nation-building and kingmaking, roles we have historically been uncomfortable with.

THE UN-IMPERIALISTS

At the 2003 World Economic Forum in Davos, Switzerland, European representatives suggested that U.S. pressure on Iraq was motivated by selfish empire building rather than a genuine interest in world security and human welfare. On January 26, Colin Powell responded this way:

> I don't think I have anything to be ashamed of, or to apologize for, with respect to what America has done for the world. We have gone forth from our shores repeatedly over the last hundred years—we've done this as recently as the last year in Afghanistan—and put wonderful men and women at risk, many of whom have

lost their lives. And we have asked for nothing [in] return.

In a television appearance where he was asked how it felt to represent a country perceived by some as "the Satan of contemporary politics," our secretary of state elaborated this way:

Far from being the Great Satan, I would say that we are the Great Protector. We have sent men and women from the armed forces of the United States to other parts of the world throughout the past century to put down oppression. . . . All in the interest of preserving the rights of people. And when all those conflicts were over, what did we do? Did we stay and conquer? No. We built [our enemies] up. We gave them democratic systems. . . . Did we ask for any land? No. The only land we ever asked for was enough land to bury our dead.

The United States is not an empire-grabbing nation. This central lesson of American history is often overlooked abroad, but it is a basic truth about U.S. foreign policy. It reflects the reluctance of everyday citizens in our country to intervene in other people's lives.

If it so chose, the United States could dominate world business and politics to a much greater extent than it currently does. Over the last two decades, the United States has grown economically at up to twice the rate of other major developed nations. Since 1970, America has created fifty-seven million new jobs; during that same period the entire European Union (which has a larger population) created just five million. The United States now produces 30 percent of all global GDP, up from 22 percent in the late 1980s. Half of all Internet traffic takes place in the United States, and three quarters of all recent Nobel Prize winners in the sciences live and work here. America's population continues to swell, while Germany, Italy, Japan, and other industrial countries are in serious population decline. The U.S. military now so overshadows any other force on the planet as to be in a class entirely by itself. Historian Paul Kennedy has characterized the power disparity between the United States and the rest of the world as without precedent in human history.

But Americans are reluctant dominators, and they have resisted the temptation to exercise their hyper-power. There is a deep, healthy, isolationist strain in our national soul, a strong desire to remain apart from the cabals and blood squabbles of the Old World. The United States was born in a reaction *against* empire, and Americans, who adhere naturally to a creed of "live and let live," still strongly prefer to tend their own gardens in quiet, rather than getting involved in any form of active imperialism.

Many Europeans seem incapable of understanding this fundamental fact of American disinterest in global manipulation. When European critics chime over and over that the U.S. police action against Iraq is just an "oil grab" they are simply projecting from their own national experiences. Europe has an ugly history of fighting maniacally over things like oil, land, coalfields, harbors, population groups, industries, entire colonies and other resources linked to wealth and power. Europeans almost never take up arms over matters of principle. They hardly ever wage war for ideals. They've rarely shed blood for liberty, self-determination, property rights, or the freedom to be left alone.

The United States, on the other hand, fights *mostly* for these sorts of principles. America's all-time bloodiest struggle—our Civil War—was precisely a battle of competing idealisms. Northerners were offended by the wickedness of slavery, and adamant to defend the unity of the nation. Southerners were contending for their right to a distinctive regional culture. Our citizens fought this dreadful war among themselves basically over matters of moral right.

Later U.S. warfighting likewise had little to do with self-aggrandizement. When the United States defeated fascism in Europe and Japan, it had no interest in making these lands dependencies. Rather than building a subject empire, the United States launched the Marshall Plan to speed its former enemies toward prosperity and independence. Several decades later, when the United States wore out aggressive communism, Americans didn't try to dominate their former opponents in Russia and eastern Europe—we welcomed them into the family of decent nations and the fraternity of economic freedom.

More recently, the United States intervened in the Balkans—the very backyard of the inert, paralyzed Europeans—to put an end to genocide. There were great risks in this course, and little or nothing for the United States to gain economically or politically from protecting the Albanians, Bosnians, and other easy prey from aggressors. But Americans loathe bullies, and are quick to defend helpless underdogs.

In Iraq, Americans acted partly out of disgust and anger at the savagery of Saddam Hussein and his henchmen toward neighboring peoples and innocent Iraqi citizens. Americans also acted in defense of their own peace and liberty. At the Army barracks in Iraq where I watched planning for the final battle of Samawah, a soldier had taped an "I Love NY" T-shirt onto a wall outside the main operations room. I saw images of the Twin Towers hand drawn on the sides of trucks, and on bombs. I saw bumper stickers paying tribute to the "NYPD" plastered on American Humvees across Iraq. One of the U.S. military units that camped in the Kuwaiti desert before entering the war zone called its assembly area "Camp 93" in honor of the passengers who fought hijackers aboard United Airlines Flight 93. These were signs of the reverence Americans feel for men and women who perish in the cause of their nation, and reminders that many millions of our citizens are willing to fight and die rather than take a foreign bit in their mouth.

At age thirty-two, Gregory Kolodciejczky may be the oldest private in the 82nd Airborne. He's in that position because he decided to start a brand new career as a paratrooper after September 11. Prior to that he worked for the fire department in New York City. When the Twin Towers collapsed, fourteen firefighters from his station were killed. A desire to honor the memory of those dead friends motivated him to join the Army, and he believes that by fighting in Iraq he is protecting Americans from future acts of terror.

This was certainly not a war over oil. Saddam's regime was perfectly happy to sell us all the oil we would take. Nor was this a war of conquest or occupation; the second Iraq is stabilized into a position of peace and international responsibility, Americans will race home from that country just as fast as jet turbines will carry them. This contest was a war in defense of freedom—our own freedom, the freedom of Iraqis, and the freedom of other men and women around the globe who cherish the chance to live in peaceful independence.

MORAL FORCE

It may happen quickly, or it may take a while, but in the end, Iraq will join the growing list of nations that have been elevated by falling to the mercies of the United States. Like Germany, Japan, Russia, Serbia, and now—a work in progress—Afghanistan, it is Iraq's fate to be *defeated into prosperity* by the Americans. In losing this war, the land of the Tigris and Euphrates has initiated its own blossoming. There is not the slightest doubt that Iraq will be a vastly safer, wealthier, and happier land ten years from now.

If the stars align, and Iraqis work hard, their nation could even follow the kind of rags-to-riches path that remade Chile, Taiwan, the Czech Republic, and other countries under America's protective gaze. For those of you to whom this sounds unbearably rosy, go dig out some microfilm of the *New York Times* in your local public library, and see what conventional wisdom had to say about the banana republics of Latin America, or the Iron Curtain nations, or squalid Asia just a couple of decades ago. Wonders happen.

One of the clear lessons of the Iraq War is the continuing utility, and morality, of righteous application of U.S. military force in our unstable world. "Saddam's fall and the American military operation's great success has had a real sobering effect on the Middle East. It's a wake-up call," observes Scott Lasensky, a Middle East expert at the Council on Foreign Relations.

The weekend after Baghdad fell, Islamic hard-liners like Hashemi Rafsanjani of Iran were suddenly suggesting, for the first time since the ayatollahs made hostages of the U.S. embassy personnel in Tehran, that perhaps

Iran should hold a popular referendum or consult an advisory panel about restoring ties with the United States. Amazing how a glimpse of the gallows can bring even chronic offenders to their senses.

This effect was seen far beyond the Middle East. In the weeks before the Iraq War, North Korea's Kim Jong Il, another mad autocrat who is estimated to have killed two million of his own people in the 1990s, seemed determined to push the world to the brink of nuclear exchange. He baldly threatened the Japanese, the South Koreans, and the United States throughout the winter, and actually launched missiles and fighter jets in two or three to-the-brink provocations.

But on April 15, with Saddam statues tumbling all across Iraq, the Korean blood brother of Iraq's Father of all Dictators suddenly had a change of heart. He agreed to negotiate with the United States and his neighbors over North Korea's rogue nuclear program.

"This is the most positive statement since this crisis started," summarized South Korean researcher Paik Hak-soon. "Its timing shows North Korea is really shocked by what has happened in Iraq." South Korea's top-ranking security adviser, Ra Jong-il, agreed that America's military triumph convinced the North Korean regime that "it wasn't in an advantageous position internationally," and therefore ought to be less inflexible.

Score one for the "Give War a Chance" faction. And deduct one from the team insisting that "War Never Settles Anything."

———

The number of Americans firmly opposed to the Iraq War was never more than a small minority, albeit one with a disproportionate attachment to the ear of our major media. While I was in Kuwait and Iraq, U.S. soldiers regularly asked me why so much of the country seemed to be opposed to what they were doing. I suggested that this was a news-generated misimpression. It happened I was doing lots of radio interviews by satellite phone during my first weeks in the Middle East, including many listener call-in shows, and I assured the soldiers that the vast majority of everyday citizens I heard from in these forums were very supportive of our troops.

I got a little taste of this firsthand twenty days after I returned home, when I was asked to speak at a "support the troops" rally in my home village. On a cold, drizzly April Saturday, about one hundred fifty people came out for singing, prayers, and speeches from former soldiers, family members, and one undernourished journalist. Perhaps the most moving set of remarks came from Laurie Selleck, an art professor who lives in our town and has two sons in the Army, one of them serving with the 3rd Infantry Division in the thick of things on the northern front in Iraq. "I can't watch the TV images, but I can't *not* watch them either," she stated with a mother's agony. "I am proud and I am terrified. I am also being reminded of the strength of the human spirit, and of the things that are important to me."

During my time away, my wife Ann got a full immersion in the lot of the military family. She did not find it easy. One day, for instance, she got a call at home from a total stranger in Colorado who was a subscriber to my magazine and had become a regular listener to my national radio dispatches. I had missed a scheduled call-in (due to fighting or a dust storm, probably), and he had gotten himself into a worry over the idea that I was dead or missing in Iraq. It wasn't hard for him to infect my wife with the same panic bug.

Even more than the separation and the stress of danger, one of the hardest things to cope with, Ann later reported, was the uncertainty—simply not having any idea where your loved one is situated. Because of the importance of operational secrecy, families of the military involved in this war often did not know if their husbands or children were in Kuwait, or Turkey, or Iraq, or at sea; whether they were in the north or south of the country; in combat or in a command post; flying missions or performing maintenance. Ann quickly joined the e-mail loops that military wives use to support each other and share tidbits of information gleaned from indirect sources. She became expert at reading between the lines of reports from military spokesmen and fellow embedded journalists, and pieced together clues from many sources as to where I was, who I might be with, and where I could be headed.

At our local rally, Laurie Selleck suggested three practical things that Americans can do if they want to help neighbors and friends who have family members in a war zone.

> First, listen to them, let them have ups and downs, let them rest at times, let them panic, let them have their silence when they need it, and a voice when they have something to say. Don't tell them to get away from it, or to think of something else. Peace for them can only begin when their loved one is home.
>
> Second, rally around our troops and focus on them. They do their job with precision, dedication, and honor. We cannot afford to question what they are doing. They need us with them; they deserve us to be with them.
>
> Number three, when it's all over, acknowledge all that we have experienced. That day when our sons return, celebrate with us. Let us all celebrate with the same intensity and the same focus that we have given to the war, because for many of us, that day will truly be the best day of our lives.

Laurie closed her remarks by describing an exchange she was replaying constantly in her mind during those difficult weeks when her son was deep in combat and completely out of touch. She had watched a CNN interview with another soldier's mother who was struggling in ways very similar to her own. It happened that the network had a correspondent with the exact unit this mother's son was part of, and they delivered a short e-mail to her boy in which she stated: "I feel so out of control. I can't protect you anymore, and I am afraid." The soldier answered his mother back with one simple sentence: "Mom—it's my turn now to protect you."

ARMED HUMANITARIANS

Clearly one result of the second Iraq war is a further deepening of America's respect and affection for her fighting forces. I thought of this every time John Abizaid popped up during my time in Iraq. Lieutenant General Abizaid was the right-hand man of CentCom Commander Tommy Franks during the war, and as an Arab-American and fluent speaker of the Arabic language, he is sure to be an important U.S. military leader in the Middle East in coming years. I first met Abizaid back in 1998, when the magazine I edit produced a special issue on America's military academies. He was then commandant of the U.S. Military Academy at West Point, and impressed me strongly as a blunt, witty, no-nonsense, soldier's soldier.

"People say West Point is turning into Penn State," he gesticulated during one of our academy interviews, "but there are no civilians walking around here in beads and sandals. We are not training people to be doctors and lawyers and candlestick makers—we're training them to be soldiers. They are not college students; they take college courses in the process of becoming officers in the Army."

But the thing I most remember when I see Abizaid representing his country in the Middle East these days is this interesting fact: The year before he entered West Point (he graduated in 1973) military service was so out of fashion in our country that the Point had to accept every single minimally qualified applicant just to get that year's class filled. That seems almost impossible today, when competition to enter our military academies has become so stiff they are now as selective as our most elite private colleges.

Abizaid and his contemporaries at the top of today's U.S. officer corps have lived through a sea change. When they came in, the military was at its absolute nadir in terms of public regard and support. During our interviews with him, the general rather bitterly recalled the time he visited Boston College for a football game in the early '70s and was saluted by Beantown college students with a Nazi "Sieg Heil." Disrespect for the military was quite common during those bleak days of Vietnam, flower power, riots, and acid, not so many years ago.

But beginning around the early days of the Reagan administration, this all began to change. Public respect for our men and women in arms has not only been restored, it stands near its highest level ever. Gallup reports that the percentage of Americans expressing "a great deal" or "a lot" of confidence in the military rose to 79 percent in 2002 (at the same time confidence in many other institutions has sagged). The American public now finds military officers more trustworthy than judges, clergymen, accountants, bankers, journalists, members of Congress, or lawyers.

Back in 1975, only 20 percent of young Americans (eighteen to twenty-nine) told the Harris Poll they had a great deal of confidence in military leaders. In April 2003, on the other hand, a large poll of college undergraduates conducted by the Harvard Institute of Politics found that 75 percent trust the military "to do the right thing" either "all of the time" or "most of the time." Two-thirds of the students said they supported the Iraq War. Today, there aren't many students at Boston College who would flip a Nazi salute to a soldier. And if one did, there's a pretty good chance someone next to him would flip back a rather different salute in response.

One soldier I met in Iraq personifies this generational shift crisply within his own family. Lieutenant Rob Gillespie, one of many smart officers I came across in the 82nd Airborne, grew up on Long Island. He describes his grandmother as a veteran protester at the White House on behalf of liberal causes. His father was a "draft dodger" during the Vietnam War. Raised in a household of do-gooders and *Village Voice* subscribers, Gillespie considered joining the Peace Corps himself. But for financial reasons he eventually used an Army ROTC scholarship to enroll at the University of Southern California.

During his ROTC training he crossed paths with a number of soldiers and officers just back from the Balkans. As he listened to them describe their work as part of an American fighting force that blocked mass murder, shielded the vulnerable, and brought relief to the starving and afflicted, Gillespie soon concluded that he could do more to help the oppressed and miserable of our planet as a member of the U.S. armed forces than in any other single occupation. With the idea that if he was going to jump in he should do it full-bore, he transferred from USC to West Point, and is now an up-and-coming commanding officer in the cavalry.

The spirit and idealism I saw in many of our soldiers in the Middle East is captured perfectly in a letter shared with me recently by friends in my church. Their strapping twenty-year-old son, Walter Rausch, is an Army paratrooper, has seen heavy service in Iraq, and is still there as I compose this. In mid-April he wrote his parents a thoughtful letter in which he announced, "The war is now over. I will tell you this: I am changed forever. In a way you could consider it a rebirth."

My life flashed before my eyes twice over here.
It never occurred to me how blind I was. We
take so much for granted. . . . My dearest beloved family, don't waste a single second. We
have been blessed to be raised in ways that are
true and just. We have more things than some
of these Iraqi children could possibly imagine. I
was ready to give it all over here to preserve
that if need be.

Walter describes the warm welcome he and other soldiers in the 101st Airborne received from most Iraqis,
saying, "We are heroes over here." Many of the fighters
the 101st encountered, he reports, were Arab and Islam-
ist fanatics from other countries and regions. Local Iraqis, he insists, are mostly peaceful. With all-American
generosity and goodwill he describes those around him:

Once Saddam was out of power the Iraqis
threw down their weapons and changed into civilian clothes and joined the cheering crowds.
These people have known nothing but oppression, tyranny, and (because of Saddam's greed)
poverty. . . . And though they worship God differently, they are faithful. We should not judge
the people as a whole because of a few extrem-
ists. A true Muslim is as good as a devout Chris-

tian. . . . And I am thankful that the children's innocence was preserved during most of this conflict.

Not only young Americans but also the public at large have rediscovered the honor of military service over the last year. A little more than a week after I got back from Iraq there was a poignant illustration of this here in my home city. Private Gregory Huxley of the Adirondack mountain village of Forestport, New York, was killed by enemy fire in Iraq on the day I came home. On April 17, his body arrived in a casket at the cargo terminal of the Syracuse, New York, airport. "Greg Huxley deserved more than being taken to the cargo area," New York State police investigator Jack Graham had concluded. So he did something about it.

Graham started calling fellow cop friends, and on six hours' notice they organized themselves. When members of the Huxley family arrived to retrieve their son's body, there were eight cars from the Syracuse Police and eight units of the New York State Troopers waiting. Airport operations halted when Huxley's flight touched down, and scores of people stood at concourse windows, watching with their hands over their hearts. Police officers in uniform carried the casket from the US Airways plane, and then escorted the hearse on its ninety-five-mile drive home. At every intersection the family crossed, troopers blocked traffic and stood at salute. Mo-